The Warwolf

The Warwolf

~

A Peasant Chronicle of the

Thirty Years War

Hermann Löns

Translated by Robert Kvinnesland

WESTHOLME
Yardley

Der Wehrwolf, Eine Bauernchronik

Originally published in 1910

English Translation ©2006 Robert Kvinnesland

Published by Westholme Publishing, LLC

Eight Harvey Avenue, Yardley, Pennsylvania 19067

ISBN 10: 1-59416-026-0

ISBN 13: 978-1-59416-026-4

www.westholmepublishing.com

Printed in United States of America

I dedicate this translation to my eldest son, Arne, and thank him for his efforts in helping me see this project come to fruition.

I would also like to acknowledge my good friend, Steve Biederman, for his invaluable feedback and encouragement.

Contents

Translator's Preface

The period of German history known as the Thirty Years War (1618-1648) can be described as an attempt by the German Protestant princes to remove themselves from the political and religious yoke of the Holy Roman Empire, as epitomized by the Catholic Hapsburg ruling elite. Foreign powers, especially France and Sweden, found political and economic advantages to be gained at the expense of both sides, making a prolonged and unconventional conflict inevitable. The general disorganization of the collective nobility in Germany and the range of religious and economic motives of opportunistic individuals and various strongmen and power brokers spelled disaster for the nation, especially its peasantry. The latter would be for three decades at the mercy of numerous domestic and foreign armies-many of which were comprised of mercenaries who, unchecked by local authorities and unpaid for long periods, ruthlessly scoured the countryside. Added to this mayhem was the general lawlessness of bands of marauders and desperate mobs of the newly displaced and impoverished. The loss of life during the Thirty Years War has been estimated at one-fifth the German population (some 21 million in 1618), while many authorities contend that the number is closer to one-third, including those who perished in battle or from disease, deprivation, and rapine. Such trauma upon civilian populations would not be matched for another 300 years, until the 20th century's world wars, which some historians have called "The Second Thirty Years War."

The results of the Thirty Years War upon Europe are briefly (and admittedly too simply) summarized as the decline of the Hapsburg Dynasty and any viable semblance of a Holy Roman Empire, a greater degree of religious toleration between Catholics and Protestants (in so much as the peace of Westphalia marked the end of what might be termed "religious" wars, but also the beginning of a separation between Austria and Northern Germany among religious lines), and political settlements and alliances which would make France the dominant continental power for centuries to come. Focusing upon Germany alone, the Thirty Years War was unparalleled in its deleterious effects upon agriculture, industry, and commerce. The tremendous loss of life, and especially the vicissitudes endured by those who survived, would be indelibly etched upon the German psyche.

Yet for all the nonfiction resources available, it is in Hermann Löns' historical novel, *Der Wehrwolf* (*The Warwolf*), first published in 1910, where the human perspective is made manifest; the tragedy and horrors of war in general and these times in particular. The novel chronicles the life of Harm Wulf and his North German farming community's struggle for survival and how Wulf and his fellow farmers are forced to make difficult choices in order to protect their homes and families. An immediate bestseller in Germany, Löns' novel remains in print in Germany and other European countries nearly a century after it first appeared and has sold more than one million copies.

Born on August 29, 1866 in Kulm, West Prussia, Hermann Löns, the son of a schoolteacher, spent his university years studying medicine and natural sciences. But the failure to complete his education caused a falling out with his family, and so he pursued poetry and journalism as a livelihood. His personal and professional life remained in turmoil with job instability, a divorce from his first wife, and bouts with alcoholism and depression. In 1901, he began to establish his reputation as "Poet Of The Heath" with the publication of *My Golden Book* and *My Green Book*. Later that decade, he turned to writing short stories and novels which encompassed themes and symbolism of ancient Germanic and Christian folklore, naturalism, and peasant life, particularly the landscape, wildlife, and people of his native Lüneburger Heath of Lower Saxony. With the outbreak of World War I, Hermann Löns volunteered for military service at the age of 48. He was killed in frontline battle near Loivre, France, on September 26, 1914.

CHAPTER 1

~

The Heathland Farmers

In the beginning the heathland[1] was desolate and unsettled. By day the eagle had dominant say over the skies, by night the owl. Bear and wolf were lords of the land and held sway over every other creature. No man challenged them; a few wretched primitives were content to eke out their subsistence by hunting or fishing, and gladly avoided contact with those beasts.

Then one evening other people arrived, folk of bright face and flaxen hair. They came with horse and wagon, kith and kin, hound and poultry. The heath suited them, for they had come from a place where ice was still on the ponds in May, and the snow fell again already in October. Every man sought a homestead for himself, then built upon it a broad house with pointed roof, covered in reeds and sod, and whose gables boasted a pair of colorful wooden horse heads.[2]

Each farm lay off on its own. Rearmost on the heath lived Heinke; his neighbor was Hingst; next followed Marten, and

1. *Haid* is a variation of *heide*, translated as "heath" or "moor." Geographically they can be considered equivalents, but for the purpose of this book I will usually use heath and its variations to signify the meadows, hills and lightly wooded dry areas, but moor or break for those areas of bogs, marshes, and/or thick woods.

2. A horse's head was considered a powerful talisman among ancient Germanic peoples, believed to ward off enemies and evil spirits. Horse head gables were considered an act of homage to the gods, securing their blessings upon the dwelling and its inhabitants.

1

then Hinnig; thereafter Hors, then Bock and Bolle and Otte and Katz and Duw and Specht and Petz and Ul, as they were all called. Finally Wulf, a large man with merry eyes and resounding voice, who settled near the break where the bogs, marshes and deep woods began.

The Wulfstead had the best pastureland of all the farms, but that farmer[3] also had the most business with bear and wolf, and with the savages who lived beyond the break. But that suited him fine, and his sons no wit less; the livelier things got, the better they liked it! And thus they grew into fellows built like trees, with hands like bear paws, yet nonetheless liked by all for their forthright nature and merry disposition as they faced the world with little guile and much laughter.

These traits served them well, and their children, and their children's children; for it occurred often enough that things got wild in the moors. Strange folk sometimes trekked through, and the heathlanders had to stay keenly vigilant, lest they be overrun.

Thus their numbers grew from century to century in Ödringen, as the village came to be called. They stood firm and repelled their enemies outright, or hid the women, children and livestock in a walled fortress deep within the break, and then set upon the interlopers by raid and ambush until the foe once again made himself scarce.

The men of the Wulfstead always came to the fore. Sometimes one of them would fall with an arrow in the neck or a spear in the chest; but another would always survive to keep the name going.

Meanwhile they put ever more land to the plow and turned the heath into meadows and pastures. The farmstead

---

3. To the modern English reader, the words farmer and peasant carry a somewhat less heroic connotation than words like freeman, yeoman, and the like. I find it apt that in the German language *bauer* also means builder, for what is the farmer if not the builder of the nation? It is this connotation that I encourage the reader to bear in mind.

tallied ten buildings and lay like a castle behind wall and moat among the oak hedges, and whose large farmhouse contained no lack of weaponry and all sorts of equipment.

A dozen heavy silver plates sat on the firewall shelf next to the hearth in the flett.[4] When the mountain farmers had sent a messenger to the heathland farmers, asking for assistance in expelling the Romans from the country, a son of the Wulfstead set out too. Even as an old man, he still had to laugh whenever he recalled the time that Varus and his legions were driven from the country, hounds hard at their heels.[5]

"Boy, that was some sport!" said the old man. "How we drubbed those slinking dogs! I myself smote about twenty of 'em, my cudgel banging like thunder off their metal skullcaps. I kept some of those shiny bowls as souvenirs, and don't they look fine there!"

The heathlanders had barely finished with the Romans when along came the Frank, who was as tough as black leather. Send him off with a backful of blows today, he nevertheless returned tomorrow. A Wulf was there when Widukind made mincemeat of a Frankish force at Suntel;[6] but two from

4. Flett, "hearth room," the first main living area at the end of the entrance hallway in farmhouses of this North German type.

5. The Battle Of Teutoberger Forest (present-day Detmold, Germany) 9 A.D., where Hermann (called Arminius by the Romans, a young Germanic noble who had been schooled in Rome and served as citizen knight in their army) and his Cheruscan tribesmen defeated three Roman legions and stopped the Empire's advance into Germania. Some historians consider it on par with Marathon and Tours as one of the most decisive battles in Western Civilization, for it marked the end of Roman advancement into Northern Europe.

6. 782 A.D. Widukind was the foremost leader of rebellion against Charlemagne until he was captured and forced to submit to baptism in 785. In return for his submission he was named Duke of Saxony and ceased all rebellion. According to some sources, he thereafter remained loyal and led so Christian a life that his name is included on the list of saints. He was killed in battle in 807, and his monumental tomb can be seen to this day in Enger near Herford, although it is doubtful his body is actually interred there, since the memorial slab has been dated circa 1100 A.D.

the Wulfstead were among the men that Charlemagne butchered like sheep at Verden.[7] Afterwards, when all who could bear arms sought revenge, three Wulfs joined in; they never returned.

However, the heath folk finally admitted: "One man alone can't outstink a dung heap!" and succumbed to the inevitable. They paid their taxes, swore off the old gods Wodin and Frigge, got baptized, and with the passing of time became respectable Christians—especially considering how one villager was beheaded after he went up onto Hingst mountain and sacrificed a white horse to the old gods, according to the ancient ways.[8]

Outwardly they appeared to be subjugated, and even tolerated a Frankish cavalier as their overlord. But inwardly they remained of old. Whenever rebellion broke out in the Holy Roman Empire, they rode over the heath in the dewy morn, set fire to the castle from all four corners, and slew everything that sported a beard.

Yet in the long run it mattered little. Through force and guile the foreign lords stripped them of one right after another, until they were finally all rent-owing tenant farmers. All except the Wulfstead, whose heir possessed a letter of privilege as mounted freeman, because once a Wulf had saved Duke Billung from his enemies. Thus whenever the Cloth or

7. "The Blood-Trial at Verden" where 4,500 Saxons believed to be ringleaders of pagan rebellion were beheaded by Charlemagne in 782 A.D., in revenge for what occurred at Suntel and as a show of power in his effort to unite all Germanic tribes under the Christian faith. The reader may also be interested in Hermann Löns' short story, *Die Rote Beeke* ("The Red Brook").

8. The horse was considered sacred by ancient Teutonic peoples, and horse sacrifice has been chronicled as far back as the Vedic literature of India (circa 1000 B.C.). The sacrifice of a white or champion horse was believed to increase good livestock, male children, and wealth. Among Northern Europeans at this time, it was also considered a pledge of loyalty to the old gods in defiance of the new religion.

the Sword[9] attempted to bring the Wulfstead under vassalage, the Wulf clan had the means to protect themselves.

Yet they too had dire moments of distress, for when war stirred in the land, so did marauders. Whenever the farmer took plow to field, spear and crossbow were likewise at hand. More than once he and his farmhands grabbed a pair of robbers and made short work of them. Times being what they were, he gave such things no further thought; his eyes remained bright and disposition merry.

When the farmers adopted the new faith and had no further use for the local priest, the head of the Wulf clan was sent to explain the situation; for the priest was a good old man, and the farmers believed that no one else was better suited to gently break the news to him than Harm Wulf, a fellow whose favorite expression was "all things must pass" (often heard as he clubbed his way through the wolf pits,[10] laughing all the while).

Afterwards came times when even Wulf's brow grew sharp, his eyes darkened, and his laugh was not so loud. That was the year 1519, when the Bishop of Hildesheim[11] and the Duke of Braunschweig combed the land,[12] and the heathland farmers shed some hair thereby. In Burgdorf the "red cock

9. Cloth or Sword, clergy or nobility; i.e. religious or secular authorities.

10. Trenches or pits were dug around farms as protection against wolves. This passage is apparently a wry comment on how Harm Wulf's persuasiveness stemmed from more than words alone. For those curious as to the appearance of these types of pits, investigate the etchings of Johann Elias Ridinger (1698-1767), especially *Der Wolf in der Grube zu fangen mit dem Schafe* (Catching The Wolf in a Pit with The Sheep).

11. Princebishop Johann IV, nicknamed "Hans Magerkohl" (Johnny Meagre-Cabbage) for his austere rule and tax levies.

12. Hildesheim–Stift Feud (1518–23). What started as a concern over revenues between Bishop Johann IV and some members of the Stift nobility (championed by Duke Heinrich of Braunschweig) soon escalated into a destructive war.

crowed loudly," as the saying went;[13] a Wulf, who had married into a landed small farming clan there, returned to the Wulfstead in poverty and soon died from a broken heart, for the Braunschweiger soldiers had ravaged his young wife.

A troop of those rabble even came as far as the Wulfstead, but since they numbered only twenty, they never found their way back. The farmer and his sons and fieldhands planted them deep within the bogs.

Later on, a time came when Wulf's son also had little cause for laughter. On the ninth of July in the year 1553, a great encounter occurred on the fowlers' fields[14] near Sievershausen between Braunschweigers and Saxons on one side, Kalenbergs and Branderburgers on the other.[15]

Both before and after the battle, events took a terrible toll on the healthland. The Wulf clan got early wind and hid the women, children, livestock and everything of monetary value within the break. The men banded together with the other farmers, and whenever they encountered foot soldiers or horsemen, fierce fighting ensued. Over two hundred were shot or beaten to death by the farmers. As they buried them, Farmer Wulf said with a derisive laugh: "A man should always do his work joyfully, especially when it brings profit," referring to the weapons and cash the soldiers had on them.

13. A red cock symbolizes fire, especially when caused by warfare or civil conflict.

14. *Vogelherde*, "fowling-floor;" a section of land (usually on the edge of a forest) where 6- to 10-foot hillocks would be built up in diameters of 30 to 50 feet so that fowlers could trap their quarry. Refer to the aforementioned Johann Elias Ridinger, especially "Fowler Heading To The Fowling-Floor With His Gear."

15. A Heidelberg League force commanded by Duke-Elector Maurice of Saxony defeated Count Albrecht Alcibiades of Brandenburg at Sievershausen, but the Duke was assassinated during the campaign.

Even during hard times, the Wulf clan would not easily lose their clear eyes and bright laugh; truly difficult and frightening things had to happen for them to become otherwise.

And so they did. In the year of 1623 all sorts of forebodings arose concerning the ever-spreading war that the Emperor was waging with the Bohemians over the new faith. A great number of wondrous signs appeared: roses bloomed with double-decked flowers; bread was purported to have bled; the field paths were littered with jellylike globs which folk called "star sniffles;"[16] for three straight days in July a swarm of irridescent dragonflies passed through the heathlands, followed by a like amount of butterflies; there were more stillbirths among the livestock than normal; mice bred in immeasurable quantity; birds of pestilence and death[17] which were rarely seen in these environs now appeared; fiery images of men shone in the heavens; and a falling star gave the appearance of a sword.

By these signs many people predicted War, Famine, Fire, and Pestilence. Indeed, it was not long before a great plague broke out, especially in the cities where people lived in close proximity and mixed with all sorts of strangers. In order to dissuade the wrath of God, great trains of half-naked men and women with chains around their necks walked behind a

16. *Sternschnuppen* is the original text, which commonly means meteoroids. But in the dialect glossary of the earlier editions (*Eugen Diederichs Verlag*) of *Der Wehrwolf*, the term is described (and I translate it here) as "gelatinous masses, possibly the fallopian entrails of frogs that had been regurgitated by polecats and herons." This leads me to believe that *schnuppen* is actually a dialect variant or possible misprint of *schnupfen*, hence I have translated the term as "star sniffles," which makes more logical (and visual) sense in the context of earlier edition's glossary notes.

17. Northern forest and mountain species like the crossbill, the nutcracker, and the waxwing. They will sometimes undertake a "disruptive" migration to more temperate areas when food supplies run low in their natural habitats.

Cross, screaming and crying as if senseless, whipping their backs with cords until the blood flowed, and singing for God's mercy.

As Harm Wulf, heir to the Wulfstead, was driving a wagonload of sod to the city, he encountered such a train with aggravation; he had inexperienced horses at the helm, and they violently tried to veer off the road as the crazy folk noisily approached.

Afterwards, though, he had to laugh. It just looked too foolish when they all suddenly threw their arms into the air and sang out:

> *"Ho, hold up your hands,*
> *So God turns the Plague from us!*
> *Ho, stretch out your arms,*
> *So God takes pity on us!"*

"What a ridiculous song!" he mused, and then continued along the road, whistling his favorite folk tune, the Brambleberry Song.[18]

---

18. *Das Brombeerlied*, variations of which have been known throughout German-speaking nations since the 16th century, encompassing the ever-popular theme of young lasses going out to pick berries in the woods, or to reap in the fields, and their subsequent (often amorous) adventures with the young lads that they encounter.

CHAPTER 2

~

The Mansfelders

As he walked through the heathland the following morning, Wulf chuckled to himself; but not about the flagellants—he had already forgotten about them.

He thought about what his father said, namely, that it was about time for him to marry and take over the farm. And he thought about Rose Ul.

For she was promised to him, the prettiest girl far and wide, with whom he always loved to dance at the harvest festival, and the only child of the Ulstead. That was why he laughed.

He twirled a mayflower[19] (which he had plucked from the old embankment in the woods) between his teeth as he gazed across the heath that was very green for the young birch arbor and resplendent from the sun.

A man approached from the direction of the break, between the high juniper shrubs. He stopped and pointed at

Mansfelders, soldiers under the command of Peter Ernst von Mansfeld, a mercenary from Luxembourg, who fought on the side of the Bohemians for the Protestant cause. Initial success against Tilly (1622) was short lived, and his undisciplined troops ran rampant, leading to his dismissal by King Frederick. He returned later with backing from Dutch and English interests, but was defeated by Wallenstein near Dessau in 1626. The term Mansfelders could also be taken to mean people from Mansfeld, a mining district and small town in central Saxony, where Martin Luther himself spent his childhood (his father owned a copper mine there).

19. *Maiblume*, mayflower or lily of the valley.

the flower Harm had in his mouth, grinned and said: "He who picks Frigga's flowers[20] can reckon his bachelorhood by hours!"

Harm laughed and shook the hand of Rose's father. Whenever he met the man he had to wonder, for this fellow was so different from all the other people Harm knew. Every word from Ul-father had a double meaning; he had a headful of jokes and nonsense, but also full of cleverness, and the reputation of a man who 'could do more than just eat bread.'

But that was merely an old wives' expression! Ul had spent three years at the college in Helmstedt; there he studied diligently, both the metaphysical and the practical, that is, spiritual subjects as well as how to treat the sicknesses of both man and beast. But when the inheritor of the Ulstead died, he had to return and take over the farm, since there were no other sons. For sport, people sometimes now referred to him as "Reverend Gabmeister".

He was nonetheless a farmer, as good as they come, except that in many things he went his own way. For example, he never attended church because (as he would say): "If you knew how sausage was made, you wouldn't eat it!" He also had the talent to rhyme whatever he said at will; no wedding ever passed without Ul-father reciting his verses, and each time something new. He had eyes that were absolutely colorless; they appeared as water. Few people could resist him, and with one of his looks, even the most vicious dog would back off.

Now he stood there grinning foolishly and said (as he noticed the firearm slung over Harm's shoulder): "Checking the boar trap again, eh?" He then laughed throatily, for the boar trap was very near the Ulstead, and when Harm was onto that task, it wasn't long before Rose also had some outdoor chore to do.

20. Frigge, Frigga (Fricka), the wife of Woden (Odin). Why the lily of the valley is referred to as her flower here is somewhat confusing, for the mistletoe is traditionally thought of as "Fricka's Flower," a symbol of love.

And so it was. As Wulf approached and saw that the trap was still open, he put three fingers to his lips and whistled like a black woodpecker. After awhile he heard a rustling behind him, and when he turned around, he caught a glimpse of something bright red behind an oak; indeed, a red skirt, which prompted a chase around the tree, then a squeal.

"Oh boy," puffed the girl as her chest heaved up and down, "you really take my breath away . . . it's nearly indecent!" But then she allowed herself to be pulled to the ground where the moss was very level and dry, and to be kissed, and she kissed back in her turn. She mused that, however many times the cuckoo called, that was how long she should live. It called but twice. "Such a lazybones!" she scolded, then laughed.

Someone called from the farm. The girl quickly sat up: "Until early evening! Mother is calling already. But don't come before supper time, because I still have so much to do." She freed herself from his embrace; Harm watched with laughing eyes, how she moved so nimbly that the red skirt waved back and forth like a flame, and how her hair sparkled like pure gold under her small cap, the binding ties of which flew just so.

Before she stepped over the breach in the hedges, she turned around once more, then disappeared. Harm's mood changed, as if the sun no longer shone so brightly and the birds no longer sang so cheerfully. But then he whistled the Brambleberry Song through his teeth and went on his way across the heath with a smile, his eyes as blue and bright as the sky above him.

Those eyes stayed bright right up to the wedding, and then became even more so. It was a large and lively wedding, even though not one man got drunk.

Although some farmers talked about how things were looking more and more dangerous throughout the realm, Harm Wulf showed little interest for fiery men in the heavens, bleeding bread, and birds of death and pestilence. Indeed, as he and his new wife were playfully shoved into their honey-moon chamber amid laughter and shrieks, of what concern would these things be to him? He took his Rose in arm and said: "I've caught myself an owl,[21] and my, what a pretty owl too!" Then he laughed at his pun.

He remained merry up to the day his Rose went to childbed, and then he laughed even more. But not so loudly, and more with his eyes; for a boy lay beside her, a prize of a boy, a real bear of a boy, a full ten pounds and handsome from the get-go!

"Well," he said to his wife on the third day, as the color returned to her cheeks, "what sort of creature is this, an owl chick or a wolf pup?" He then laughed loudly over his jest.

He laughed when he went to the fields, and he laughed when he returned. He had had a nice life earlier, but as things now stood, with such a comely wife and healthy son, well . . . that was something altogether different! He could just burst with joy, so boisterous was his mood. And even if now and then Reineke or Marten or one of the other Ödringers acted like a rooster upon seeing a fox approach, relating what had been heard in Celle or Burgdorf or Peine, namely, that war was being waged throughout the realm, and it won't be long before the heathland gets a whiff of it, Wulf-farmer whistled his Brambleberry Song while he sowed or plowed, thought about his Rose and little Hermke, and in general what a lucky fellow he was.

Hermke could already toddle along holding his mother's hand, and call out "Papa!" when he saw Harm returning from the fields. Indeed, things had progressed so that he would soon have a brother or sister.

One morning the farmer rode to town to pay his property taxes to the authorities. It was a beautiful morning: the birch

---

21. Many of the clan names originated from nature, e.g. *Ul* "owl," *Wulf* "wolf," *Bock* "goat," *Specht* "woodpecker," *Katz* "cat."

trees along the path had recently burst open; the finches argued; the meadowlarks sang; the moors were red from top to bottom for the myrtles that were blooming. Harm set his horse to a light trot, the dust kicking up lightly behind him as he thought: "the sooner I get to town, the sooner I can get back to the farm."

But he didn't arrive home until late that evening, and he came on foot.

After he had paid his taxes and returned to the inn outside of town where he had stabled his dun (in order to save toll money), it was a wild scene. A Mansfeld field captain had arrived with his troop of soldiers, and they were having a high time indeed. The men were all red in the face from beer and schnapps; amid howling, bellowing and squealing, they were taking all sorts of liberties with the camp-follower hussies who accompanied them. It was a scandal to behold! The daughter of the innkeeper and the serving girls were likewise hard-pressed. Even the old wife, who long ago had lost her looks, had to defend herself from the louts.

As Wulf-farmer headed around the house to get to the stables, he was accosted by a fellow with a red feather in his hat and a nasty looking pitch-black moustache under his long nose. The bloke hurrahed loudly, took the farmer by the arm, and kissed him on both cheeks (so that the stink of schnapps assaulted Harm's nose). He then grabbed Wulf by the shoulders and held him at arms length, laughing over his entire jaundiced face as he bellowed: "Brrrotherheart of mine! How long since we seen each other? Oh joy on joy! But this calls for a drrrink!" He dragged the confused farmer to the ordering window and shouted: "Madaaaam Hostessssss . . . two beerrrs for me and mine frrriend, who I've not seen in so long!"

The head serving girl brought the beer, but when the strange horseman pinched her arm and reached for the mugs, she shrieked and let them drop. She then signaled to Wulf with her eyes, for she was a daughter from one of the smaller houses of Ödringen and recognized him. The foreigner cursed bloody murder, but then his captain called and he had to depart.

As Harm was about to hasten on his way, Trine Reineke waved for him to come inside: "Farmer Wulf," she said, "by the blood and wounds of Christ, absolutely never converse with one of these rabble-rousers! Whoever does is then pressed into service! Look, there's Kristian Bolle. They already roped him in, that dullard! He knocked mugs 'To Brotherhood!' with each of them, and now he wears their colored armband. For all anyone knows, he'll get himself shot dead tomorrow, in the name of God or the Devil!"

The pretty girl—whose first job was as young servant on the Wulfstead—anxiously looked him in the eyes: "See to it that you get going, the sooner the better! These are not men, these are true beasts! Oh God!" she lifted her apron to her face and starting crying.

"There, there, lass," said Harm as he touched her shoulder to calm her. "All things must pass. But you're right . . . whoever hasn't mislaid something around these parts shouldn't tarry." He paid for both mugs of beer, included a tip, and then headed for the stables.

The situation there was even wilder than by the inn. Seven stable lads, one meaner looking than the next, were tormenting an old Jew, a junk dealer. They were spitting in his hands, scattering his wares, and trying to force him to eat a pork sausage. Three others were butchering a sow, another was having his way with a gypsy girl who couldn't have been more than twelve, another was lying drunk on a dung heap, and yet another had a rooster in hand and was twisting its neck.

"My God," thought the farmer, "what sort of business is this!" He pushed past the drunken men and went to the horse stall. His dun was there, but it was bridled with a lordly harness and two saddlebags. He unharnessed the horse, made a halter out of a cord, and then led it out of the stall. As he was some distance from the inn, a cavalryman with a red beard that hung over his collar rode up and challenged him about where he thought he was going with the horse.

"Why, this dun was mine from the start!" the farmer shot back. "Ferdl, Tonio, Peter, Vladislav, front and center!" shouted the red-beard. "Who owns this horse . . . this man here or Corporal Tillmann Anspach? Eh? Call him over! We'll see whose word counts for more... that of an honest soldier, fighting for the true faith, or that of some peasant who arrived on foot, but wants to depart on horse!"

Harm flushed red with anger and reached toward the trouser seam where his knife was sheathed. But then he calmed himself, for he was one against a dozen and a half; and now here came the corporal, a fellow as gaunt as a beanstalk with a scar from eye to chin, and behind him another dozen riders who looked like Satan's own cousins.

As the corporal heard what the argument was about, he shook his head, lifted two fingers into the air and swore: "As I stand here on two legs," (and he thereby lifted one foot) "I'll be damned if that's not the dun I bought on Martinmas[22] from Schlome Schmul at Cologne on the Ring for thirty solid thalers[23] and a good bottle of wine. By these words I live and die, as I am a true Christian and no Papist dog!"

Harm looked around and considered his plight: he stood between thirty or more reckless hotheads who wouldn't care if they had the blood of one more man on their hands; yet

22. St. Martin's Day, November 11th, is celebrated throughout Germany. Parades are common and at twilight groups of children with colorful lanterns go singing through the streets well into the night. Sometimes the story of St. Martin of Tours is enacted, how he tore his cloak in two and shared it with a beggar. A special meal of roast goose, the *Martinsgans*, is often served.

23. Thaler or taler: Any of various silver coins that were used as currency in Germanic countries between the 15th and 19th centuries, and from which the English word dollar stems.

they were all drunk, and if only he had been mounted on the dun already, he could have put the horse to spur and made a run for it. But in the end, the nag was not worth risking life and limb over, for the animal had a dumb habit of heeding a whistle! So if one of the soldiers got the idea in his head to whistle, then he, Harm, would end up the idiot, and his wife could wait for him until she was old and gray. Already three or four of the stable men were reaching for their knives, and a woman with black hair (from which the sweat ran down like butter) was elbowing a cross-eyed and scar-laden bloke standing next to her; she was making eyes like a wolf who scented prey.

Harm Wulf suddenly laughed: "Children and people," he cried out, "this here is some wild living! Even madder than when the Martin's Fair[24] comes to town! To a backwoods yokel, such as myself . . . who sees a new face but once every six months . . . well . . . it sets the head reeling! You're absolutely right! My dun is in the town! Yea oh yea, a man shouldn't have schnapps before noon on an empty stomach! No offense meant! To err is human, like the rooster said as he dismounted the duck. And now let's really down one, so that the meadows sway!"

"Lookie there," he shouted heartily, "here comes my old friend!" With that he put his arm around the man with the black moustache and red feather in his hat, then called towards the house: "Innkeeper! Trine, girl, hurry, hurry! Beer here!"

As the horsemen laughingly followed, he threw a thaler on the window sill and sang: "I have yet a thaler, it needs to be drunk up!" He knocked mugs with everyone and began telling jokes, but kept an eye on his back and his lips dry, tossing the beer and schnapps over his shoulder against the wall.

---

24. For the two to three days before St. Martin's Day, a lively fair is held in many towns.

The pretty Trine couldn't serve the drinks fast enough, so festive was the crowd. But when she returned for the eighth time, Wulf-farmer was gone.

He had told one of Ul-father's crudest jokes, and as the drunken band laughed themselves crooked (some of them translated for the others who didn't understand the dialect, until all were slapping their thighs and bellowing like oxen), Harm whispered something to the hostess; she then called out: "Dinner's ready! Everybody come to eat!" They all stood up to go inside, and Wulf pressed himself behind a tree.

Luckily, he was able to make his escape. A stable man who got in his way took a fist under the heart and fell into a latrine without a word. The red-beard asked him: "Brrrother, dear brother, another drrrrrink?" but Harm shoved him headforemost into the hedges. As the black-haired gypsy girl was about to shout an alert, he gave her the evil eye and held his knife to her face. At first she turned as white as a sheet, then nervously laughed and said: "Oh, such strong a man, preeeetty man!" He just shoved her out of his way and sprang into the bushes.

When he reached the undergrowth, he stopped to catch his breath; gnashing his teeth and clenching his fist, he cursed: "If only I . . . I should have . . . if I was a single man, they would have paid me what the dun was worth, those swine!"

But he calmed down again, once back in the heath within sight of his farm. As his wife came running up to meet him, totally pale in her face and dark under her eyes (for he had never stayed away so long), he could again smile, and tell her what happened to him as if it were only a practical joke.

But later, as he lay in bed and relived everything in his head, he clenched the fingers of both hands. If not for his wife sleeping so peacefully beside him, as if there were nothing on earth but angels, he would have gladly cursed out loud; just like his father-in-law, when in his foulest mood: "You should break your neck on that stupid horse!"

Instead, he lay there motionless in the stifling heat. That morning he had whistled the Brambleberry Song between his teeth as he rode to town, but now? Now he lay there thinking about the song that the red-bearded fat man bellowed in his face, the same bloke he later threw headlong into the hedges. Like a senseless beast he bellowed:

> *The Mansfelder is coming,*
> *Hurrah, hurrah!*
> *The Mansfelder is coming,*
> *Hurrah, hurrah!*
> *Tru-dee Ri-dee Rah-lah-lah-lah,*
> *The Mansfeld man is here,*
> *Huzzah!*

CHAPTER 3

～

The Braunschweigers

The following day, Harm's eyes grew bright again as little Hemke played hop-hop-rider on his knee, crowing happily and pulling on his father's ears. But later, while Wulf was sowing, he couldn't keep his mind off of what had happened at the inn.

"The Devil take it all," he thought, "that I had to give up a horse for nothing, and nothing again, to the first scalawag that happened along. And then buy a round of drinks, to boot!"

He thought long and hard about these things, and since he had business at the Ulstead, he talked it over with his father-in-law.

"Tcha," said Ul-father as he spat in the fire, "that's some nonsense! Even though you can afford the loss, a horse isn't chickenfeed, and too dear to just give away. Tell you what . . . I have business in Celle anyway, and as you say, that's where those men were heading. I'll see what can be done. I'm in good with the lords of the court there, ever since that time our Duke came over on the hunt and laughed himself half to death over my Wild Boar Song. Perhaps you should come along too. I can't go today . . . but tomorrow."

The next morning they headed out. It was once again a fine day: the larks sang over the meadows and a curlew war-

Braunschweigers, soldiers from Braunschweig (often anglicized as Brunswick), one of the largest cities in Lower Saxony.

bled from the break. But the two farmers appeared ill-tempered and, as they came face-to-face with three horsemen, Harm gripped the reins tighter, while Ul-father set his pistol close by in the wagon straw. But the riders passed by, merely thanking them as they were bid a good morning.

These were three men whose faces the Devil might have envied. One of them couldn't keep his eyes off of the horse team; when Harm turned around he saw that they had stopped and were talking among themselves. But then they set to a gallop and rode straight into the heath.

Wulf-farmer and Ul-father met all sorts of other folk along the way; at first, two vagabonds, then three, then some gypsies came alongside in a covered wagon that was crawling with naked children. One of them jumped from the wagon (a girl who must have been about thirteen, yet bare as a fish) and before Harm knew it, she was sitting beside him on the saddle horse and started begging; three or four of the others busied themselves with Ul-father in the wagon.

"These brats cling worse than deer lice!" said Wulf-farmer, after they had shaken off the naked company; he then added: "The sort of folk that are now traipsing around the countryside! It's a shame that nothing is done! Soon sneak-thieves and vagabonds will be lords of the land. If things keep going like this, nothing good can come of it."

When he looked back at the gypsies, he noticed that the three horsemen had returned and were following them. This struck him as suspicious, so he put the horses to a quick pace, in order to reach the city before the riders.

It was a motley scene at the city gate. A large group of foreign soldiers were there, idling about. When the farmers asked the guard about it, they were told that this mixed collection of rabble had been recruited by Christian von Braunschweig, steward of the diocese of Halberstadt, to fight against the Imperial forces. The crowd was behaving reasonably well, for they were within range of the city's cannons; also, a unit of the duke's soldiers, under a captain, kept an eye open so that no mischief occurred. But when Harm took a look at them, he thought to himself: "Most look like refugees from the gallows, no more than one step ahead of the hangman."

In Celle they stopped at 'Towards The Golden Sun', a pub where they were well known, and had breakfast with four farmers from the Flottwede district. "We will soon see many things," reckoned the Wathlingen Burvogt.[25] "The Wienhaus nunnery has already shut its doors, and the sisters have made themselves scarce . . . otherwise, before long they might have lost the purity of their bodies or the zeal of their calling . . . perhaps both.[26] In Old Celle the scoundrelly soldiers violently robbed the farmers of their sausages and hams, and beat them, to boot! That big dairy farmer, Pieper, now lays dying in his house . . . he tried to stop them from molesting his daughters . . . then one of the blokes hit him in the head with a saber . . . and spilled his brains."

He paused and looked around, then whispered: "The man who did it . . . he vanished too! Word has it that the farmhands met him 'around the corner', as it were. Also in Wathlingen, two of those 'brothers-in-arms' gang disappeared . . . with my blessing!"

25. *Burvogt*, a community representative or town leader, village elder, or overseer.

26. The translator admits to taking liberties with the phrase: "*denn sonst könnten sie wohl bald ihr Nonnenfleisch losgeworden sein.*" When Germans speak of having the *fleisch* (flesh) for something, it connotes the aptitude, desire, or tolerance for that thing. For example, to listen to the long operas of Wagner, one needs to have *Sitzfleisch* (literally "sitting flesh"). So, while this phrase might denote the nuns' fear of being bodily violated, I believe the author's intent in using the specific word *Nonnenfleisch* also connotes the "zeal of the calling" that might be lost. Indeed, later on in this story, mention is often made regarding folks losing their faith in God due to experiencing the barbarity of the world.

"That's the thing," said a farmer from Eicklingen, "that's the thing! A man's life is no longer safe, but taxes increase! The assembly just passed a triple assessment, and reports say it won't be the last, because money is needed for armies. It's true! And even that would be tolerable, except then come these foreigners who burden us in all sorts of ways . . . that is, when they don't outright steal everything they can get their hands on! Pohlmann's son, Ludwig . . . they took his milk cow out of the pasture . . . when he asked to at least be paid for it, they laughed with scorn! And when Hein Reimers returned from the fields, why . . . he was out two good horses in the same manner! If this continues there will be no law and order at all!"

Then the Ödringers related why they had come to Celle. But everyone figured they should just write off the dun as up in smoke, because there weren't enough hours in the day for the authorities to pursue such things. But Ul reckoned he'd try anyway, so then departed.

He returned after two hours looking very deflated, hanging his head like an ailing rooster. "Yes, son," he said, "that was some business! They barked at me to keep quiet about such nonsense . . . said that they had more important things to do than go running after horses. Well, I can't say they're wrong. It's just like the second cook said . . . the way things are in the world nowadays, it's like an ant hill after the woodpecker starts a-digging. The Imperials come from one side, the Braunschweigers and Durlachers from the other . . . and our reigning Duke's concern is to not get his fingers clamped between them. Mertens reckoned that Duke George . . . whom they've promoted to regional colonel, with twenty-thousand troops under his command, by the way . . . will see to it that we don't get skinned alive. Nevertheless, you're out the dun. I hope the bloke breaks his neck on the dumb horse!"

He struck a match for his pipe, spat on the floor, and looked his son-in-law in the eye: "I don't know . . . I guess that's the way it is. Remember what your grandfather always used to say? 'Help yourself, then our Lord God will help you!' And why? The authorities have their hands full trying to maintain general order to what extent they can. Other than that, it's every man for himself. I don't know what to make of it. What are we supposed to do, for example, if a hundred or more of these vultures, like the ones milling around outside the city gate, end up near Ödringen?"

"Come," he then said, "let's go! There's nothing more to be gained here." He called to the innkeeper and paid. "Hey now!" he suddenly cried out; "Harm, boy, what's this?!" And he quickly ran out the door. As Harm followed him into the courtyard, he saw that one of the three riders from their morning encounter was leading his saddle horse out of the stall.

"Ho there!" Ul-father shouted, loosening his knife; "What do you call this?!" The stranger looked at him and laughed: "Well, I can surely inspect the horse, can't I? I told the stable boy what I was doing, and even asked him who the owner was. I'm a horse trader, since you ask . . . your horse caught my eye immediately. He's a perfect match to another one that I'm currently haggling over . . . the pair would make a lordly team. What'll you take for it?"

Wulf-farmer shook his head. "Not for sale," he said, leading the horse to the wagon. The other replied: "Well, then not . . . perhaps not today, but tomorrow might be different. Maybe you'll change your mind." And with that the trader departed.

The Ödringers saw him off with sharp eyes, and the innkeeper snapped his fingers. "Tcha, him a horse dealer!" he growled. "Whoever buys so cheaply can prosper indeed! He comes here a lot, and though he eats and drinks plenty, I'm happier to see him going rather than coming. First, because I don't like his eyes . . . and second, I saw him hanging around with that rabble from the marshes near Celle, to whom self-respecting people of means give a wide berth. Hahnebut's his name . . . Jasper Hahnebut from Botfeld, near Hannover. He's mostly seen in the company of Hans von Roden and Kaspar Reusche . . . another pair that I wouldn't trust out on the open road."

Just as they were about to head out, a great hue and cry arose from the tilting yard.[27] A farmer was being escorted between two constables, followed by his daughter, a pale girl of about seventeen years, who was crying into her apron. "Accursed spawn!" he shouted. "Those dogs should be beaten to death! I can put up with sport just like the next fellow . . . but too far is too far! Is my daughter to be molested by any louse-jacket who comes along? Well . . . that lout won't soon try it again! His eye will be hanging out of the socket for another four weeks . . . I'm only sorry I didn't knock it out of his head altogether! So now we'll see if law and justice still exist in the land . . . and whether we live in a Christian nation or under Turks and Heathens!"

A craftsman, known to the innkeeper, related the story. The farmer, a man from Boye, was taking his daughter to the doctor, for she had pains in her chest. As he and she came among the Halberstadt soldiers, they grabbed at her like she was some vagrant trollop. Her father then gave one of the blokes such a fist in the face that one of his eyes popped out. So now the situation is being investigated by the authorities. "But," he added, "they'll probably soon let him go. Word from the castle is that the Braunschweigers have been ordered to depart within the hour, or the Duke's men will put them to spur!" He looked at the farmers: "If I were you, I'd wait a bit before leaving. The soldiers are pulling out now, and not in a real good mood."

---

27. A side road or enclosed yard reserved for contests of horsemanship and/or fighting skills, especially jousts.

The Ödringers considered this sound advice and accompanied the man back into the pub. Just as the clock struck two, Ul suddenly widened his eyes and made a face as if he saw something frightening. "Come," he called, "we've got to go now. We don't have to travel the main highway . . . we can take the side roads through the heath. Suddenly I have an uneasy feeling in my gut . . . don't know why. Maybe it's just all the aggravation."

And so they started out. All was quiet by the city gate, except that all sorts of gypsies were still there. As the Ödringers were about to turn off into the heath, a call came from behind and three farmers from Engensen rode up. "G'day!" said the eldest. "Take us along. The way things are nowadays, five travel together better than two or three. Earlier we saw three men ride by who looked like they fell out of the Devil's knapsack. It's about time that Duke George scoured the land with a fine-toothed comb . . . all sorts of vermin abound." He turned and waved to a younger farmer who was riding along the main road: "Hinnerk, better head over here, lest you get bored riding alone." Thus they were six, with no worries, since each had a pistol and large knife by his side.

"Farmer Wulf," said the Engenser, "we farmers have to stick together now. In our area we've already made a pact: Gypsy and other strange folk who show up in the area are greeted immediately by the lash . . . because that lot act as spies for the marauders . . . and what else would you call these soldiers . . . showing them where goods are to be gleaned. In Ehlershausen several weeks ago they quietly hung and buried two of these blokes who took a horse from the meadows. That's simple justice, nothing more. First, they aren't proper folk . . . and second, why didn't they just stay where they belonged?"

The other farmers nodded, except Ul-father; he sat there and looked over the heathland with wide eyes, grimacing like

a demon, mumbling now and then to himself. As Harm likewise looked out over the heath, it seemed to him as if a man
jumped behind one of the stunted pines. He mentioned it to
Drewes and the Engenser directed his attention to the path,
then pointed and said: "Could well be. Here are the tracks of
one . . . two . . . three riders. I wouldn't be surprised if it was
those three suspicious blokes from before. Well, let them
come! We have our six, a good number for a thrashing."

They starting laughing and prattling loudly, acting like the
heath was a garden playground, but keeping their hands on
their pistols and their eyes peeled. They saw nothing suspicious, except that three deer suddenly bolted from behind
some pines, as if wolves were in pursuit. When they passed
that spot, they heard a stallion whinny in the bushes; the
Ödringers had a mare on the wagon team, and she appeared
to grow skittish. They looked around and boasted even louder, laughing as if senseless - all except the Gabmeister, who sat
very still and quiet, biting his lips and gazing anxiously in the
direction of Ödringen.

After they had gone on for another fifteen minutes, they
again heard the stallion bray. Suddenly Drewes waved the
others back and rode hard into the heath after something that
appeared to be running; they couldn't tell whether it was man
or beast. All at once they heard something like a scream, and
then Drewes emerged, saying: "I figured it was a wolf."

Harm, who was riding beside him, looked closely and saw
that there was fresh blood on the thick walking stick that the
Engenser had hanging on his saddle (for his right leg was a bit
short). Drewes caught the look: "It was a gypsy who had been
creeping along behind us for the past hour. No doubt playing
the spy for those three bushwhackers. But I flushed him out
and gave him a good knock. One less now . . . no other way to
handle it!"

Wulf suddenly felt uneasy about the Engenser. Granted,
the gypsies weren't civilized folk, and certainly not true

Christians (even if they did allow their children to be baptized, after a manner, for the sake of a florin[28] from the godparent sponsor). But to just strike them down like wild animals? Harm didn't want to consider it.

But he had to admit that Drewes was right, as the latter quietly said to him: "If each town has a doughty fellow who organizes all the able-bodied, and one town helps another, things will then go well. By thunder, we weren't put here to be abused by every hungry Hans and lusty Jans! I'm telling you, and thus should all men vow: 'Before I allow anyone to harm a finger on me or mine, I'd rather ride ankle-deep in blood'. Well then, adieu!" He rode off to the left with his three companions.

Wulf and Ul had barely gone a stretch further when they again heard a stallion neigh. As they stopped, they saw the three strange riders following slowly behind. "I can guess what these blokes have in mind!" said Ul-father. "Let's make like there's a tangle in the reins, then edge around behind the wagon. That way, we can greet them with a good volley if they try anything." Thus they dismounted and busied themselves with the equipment as the riders slowly approached.

As they were nearly upon them, the one whom the innkeeper said was named Hahnebut called out: "Well, are you ready to sell the horse?" as he held his rifle before him on the saddle. Wulf shook his head and replied: "Not for sale." He placed himself behind the horses and took pistol in hand, while Ul did the same. "I've got to have that horse, damn you!" shouted the man. "What's it going to be?" He made wide threatening eyes and pointed his rifle at Wulf.

At that very moment Wulf heard the Engensers approach (Drewes' saddle squeaked in a most peculiar manner) and a shot rang out before the bushwhackers could make their get-

28. Florin, any of several gold coins formerly used throughout Europe, based upon the original 13th-century coin minted in Florence, Italy.

away. The one behind Hahnebut fell forward on his horse, but managed to hold on and follow the other two, who were making like rabbits towards the moors. He soon tumbled off his mount, but then was grabbed by Hahnebut and pulled up on the saddle behind him, while his own horse ran wildly to and fro. The Engensers pursued and shot twice more.

"Looks like we came back at the right moment, boys!" laughed Drewes as he broke off the chase and came back around. "I happened to look to the rear once more and saw the louts following you. Well, one of them will have a splitting headache, at least. Too bad a fly buzzed onto my front sight as I pulled the trigger . . . made me shoot a bit high. Still, it was great sport! Those rabble surely rode off with a good pantsload of fear. And they're out that brown stallion, too!"

He clucked with his tongue and rode after the horse. "Well, Hans . . . come here. Good boy!" He held onto the halter and looked the horse up and down. "That's what I thought!" he then said. "Look here . . . isn't that Tidke Runde's mark?" He pointed to the brand on the stallion's shoulder. "Well, it certainly wasn't paid for. I tried to buy a four-year old from him the other week, but he didn't have any to spare because he had just lost one to colic. We've just earned ourselves a round of beers, so let's go to Ehlerhausen and drink it in advance. Chasing wild hares dries out a man's liver!"

There was a great hubbub at the inn when the six farmers arrived with the stallion. Runde from Wettmar was already there, complaining how someone stole his brown out of the pasture in the middle of the night. A crowd of farmers from the district and outer areas were also present, discussing the Braunschweigers. Wherever those soldiers went, mischief followed. But since they numbered only a hundred, and the farmers kept a stern eye in their direction, things weren't going too badly; especially considering that many were drunk and could barely stand on two feet. The latest troop had recently departed; the wind blew in the direction of the town, and one could still hear them bellowing in song: "Merry Braunschweigers, such are we!"

Another round of beers was to follow, but the Ödringers felt uneasy, so they departed. Ul's eyes grew ever bleaker, and neither was Harm in a good mood. The closer he got to home, the stranger he felt. As he caught sight of the stead, a farmhand came running. "Well, what's the matter?" Wulf called to him, sensing immediately that something was not right.

"Oh, boss", stuttered the hand, "the missus . . . some of those creatures came to the farm and the hens . . . they wanted to grab the hens . . . and your wife tried to stop them . . . then one of the men hit her in the stomach with his rifle . . . and there she lay . . . unconscious . . . and the child . . . it was a girl . . . it's . . . it's dead.

"Boy!" bellowed the farmer; "What about your mistress! How is she now?" The farmhand stepped back and stuttered even more: "It's not . . . a matter of life and death, according to Mother Midwife . . . it's just the after-effects . . . of shock." He walked next to the farmer: "Around two o'clock . . . that's when the ruffians came. First they demanded beer . . . then schnapps . . . and one of them went into the chicken coop . . . that's when it happened."

Duwes-mother met the farmer at the side door. "Quiet! She's asleep now. She had the fever earlier and called for you endlessly. But afterwards she fell asleep and had a good sweat." She suddenly cried: "Such an adorable girl, the little one! That it had to die before coming into the world! These dogs, these godforsaken dogs! I could watch them burn alive! And the woman barely said a harsh word to the man! She merely called out: 'Please, not the laying hens! I'll gladly give you a sausage!' And for that she now lays there and the child is dead!" She lifted a sheet that was draped across two stools.

"Look! There it is. It would have been a beautiful and healthy child!"

Harm barely looked in that direction. He had already removed his shoes and went to the bedroom. His wife slept, he could hear her breathing quietly. He got himself a glass of water and a piece of dry bread and sat on the high-backed stool near the oven. Thoughts whirled around in his head, like the swallows over the meadow. As time passed, he calmed down somewhat, but sleep was out of the question. "Drewes was right," he mulled. "Every man for himself and his own. Better a stranger's blood on one's knife, than a stranger's knife in one's blood!"

He felt like he was going out of his mind for fury. His wife . . . hit in the stomach by one of these blokes . . . his wife . . . who couldn't harm a fly. He wanted to mount his horse and ride the man down. But that's nonsense! It served no useful purpose to dwell upon how good it would be to beat and strangle the life out of the man.

He sat like that the whole night, with open eyes, staring at the alcove where his wife slept. As the owls began to hoot, the woman stirred and called softly: "Harm . . . husband?" He quickly went to the bed and took her hand in his, remaining like that until the dawn. He then sat again on a large stool and stared woodenly until his eyelids fell. But he suddenly jumped up and looked around wildly; when he realized where he was, he sighed and sat back down.

He dreamt that he had ridden out in pursuit of those men, and had come upon one . . . exactly the one he had in mind . . . who was swaying and singing the Braunschweiger song. He grabbed that one from behind and strangled him until he was blue in the face and no longer moved a finger.

Harm quietly left the bedroom and washed himself outside in a basin. The blood rang in his ears and every hair on his head tingled. So dangerous was the look in his eyes that, when Gripper approached and saw him, the dog immediately put his tail between his legs.

It was enough to drive a man crazy. There now lay his wife . . . who knows if she'll live…? And that bloke . . . that dog . . . might this very moment be swinging a beer stein and singing:

"Duke Christian takes good care of us!
Beer and spirits he shares with us!
Musicians for our leisure…
Pretty girls for our pleasure…
With our beer and with our wine,
Merry Braunschweigers, we're so fine!"

CHAPTER 4

~

The Weimaraners

It was very subdued on the Wulfstead after that. The farmer's wife slowly regained her strength, but she was no longer her former cheerful self. She remained pale and introverted, and startled at every little thing. The farmer changed too; rage and anger ate away at his heart. He had forgotten how to whistle when he worked, and when he laughed, it was as if the late autumn sun peeked from behind the clouds for only a moment.

To be sure, these were no times for whistling. Taxes were constantly on the rise, and beggars of all sorts traipsed through the land: Westphalians, Friedlanders, Lippizaners, folks who had up to this time lived in peace and freedom, but who were now reduced to vagrancy because the Mansfelders or Braunschweigers had taken all they owned, and burned the roofs over their heads, to boot.

People had shocking tales to tell, more than a human could tolerate without going mad. Harm met a woman in the middle of the moors who was singing and praying and praising God for His kindness. He found it hard to bear and took her back to the farm, where she regained her senses somewhat.

She had possessed a good farm; her husband was tortured to death, as were her three daughters and small son. This

Weimaraners, soldiers from the region of Weimar, a city in east central Germany.

drove her over the edge and now she wandered aimlessly through the land.

She ate like a wolf and spoke between mouthfuls. It was gruesome to behold, how she recalled it all without emotion, then suddenly laughed, and again prayed and sang praises to God.

The farmer was glad to see her leave, even though he felt sorry for her. But his wife became upset and took ill after hearing the strange woman's story. Three times that night she awoke with a scream, and only calmed down again when Harm took her hand and spoke to her. The next day she was so sick she couldn't get out of bed, and startled in fear whenever a door closed.

Thereafter the farmer forbade his people to talk about what was going on in the world. He remained in the house and yard to the extent that he could, and left the fieldwork to his farmhands. As much as he himself was troubled, he forced himself to laugh and whistle, for he noticed that it did his wife good and her condition slowly improved. Evenings when she brought the boy to bed and he would babble and squeal and laugh, she too could laugh along. But it was surely not the laugh she used to have, the laugh that made the farmer feel very warm under his scarf. Her father, who now visited the Wulfstead often, tried his best to cheer her up with his jests and nonsense. But it was, and remained, a half-finished task.

Since it appeared there would be no end to the bleeding, plundering, torturing and torments, the farmers around the break agreed among themselves to provide mutual alerts so that the livestock and women could be hidden. Every few weeks one of the farmers would have to send forth a rider whenever bad news came from some quarter, forcing the Ödringers to drive their livestock head over heels into the walled fort in the middle of the break, and leaving their women and servant girls in the sod huts there until the coast was again clear.

Farmer Wulf lost his best man to that task: Katz rode to the next town to warn that a large troop of Weimaraner soldiers were on the way. The next day his white horse came back, but with blood on its back and a bullet graze on its neck. And without its rider.

Up to this point, the Wulfstead saw less of the war's effects than the other farms in Ödringen, due to its remoteness. Likewise, vagabonds seldom found their way out there.

Then one autumn morning, after the first frost appeared overnight, a gypsy woman came a-begging with a half-naked baby at her breast. Ul-father wanted to loose the dog on her, but his daughter and the farmer stopped him. "Father," the farmer's wife said, "she has a child at her breast and seems half-starved!" The old man grumbled as she gave the woman warm milk, bread, and some used clothing. Grandfather Wulf, who never said much since his retirement, mentioned: "I hope you don't come to regret this, girl!"

That afternoon a Weimaraner officer and thirty men approached the farm. They came through the middle of the heathland where there was barely a path, and grandfather Wulf said: "Didn't I tell you!"

They behaved somewhat orderly, since they lacked no bread nor sausage; also, the officer saw to it that they remained sober, for they had a long march ahead of them. However the farmer had to lend them two teams of horses, despite his reluctance. And because one of the horses kicked his stable hand, giving the lad a stiff knee, Harm himself had to accompany them, regardless of the inconvenience.

At first he was just supposed to bring the horses to Burgdorf. But as they were out on the high heath, a gypsy ran up and spoke to the leader; the train changed course to Wettmar, where there were two wagons of oats that Harm was to bring along.

It was late evening when they arrived in Bisseldorf. Things here were going wildly. There were Weimaraner troops everywhere, amid such yelling and activity that Harm's mood grew downcast. The innkeeper and his wife looked as if they had been pulled from the grave. The serving girl's hair hung loose on her head, and her blouse and scarf were ripped high and low. Their children were sitting on a heap behind the baking house, petting a dog that one of the soldiers had beaten to death. Nearby sat a workman, holding his sides and spitting blood; he got a rifle butt in the ribs trying to defend the serving girl.

Wulf waited and waited, because the officer had told him: "You'll get your horses back." Around midnight, Wulf bought a mug of beer for a soldier so that he would remind the officer of his word. As Harm tried to put his money back in his pocket, the purse was ripped from his hand and, before he could do anything about it, he was thrown down towards the door. He reached for his knife, but then calmed himself and waited until the officer went to retire for the evening. As a tall man (whom the others addressed as "Colonel") headed his way, he stepped before him, removed his hat, and asked if he could now have his horses back.

"Shut your hole!" snapped the officer. "What do I care about your horses, dumb peasant!" Wulf nearly choked, but held himself in check. "Sir Colonel, the other officer gave me a hard and fast promise that my teams would be returned," he said, surprising himself at how he was able to speak so calmly. The officer grew red in the face: "Are you mad, filthy lout?!" he cried. "Are you mad?! This bloke dares to block my path! Make way!" And because the farmer didn't immediately move, the colonel slapped him in the face with the long yellow gauntlet gloves that he carried in his hand, so that it cracked loudly, and went past him.

Wulf stood stock-still and dumbfounded, barely hearing the baggage train attendant, who said: "War is war, and that's that. Console yourself, as I have. Once I too had a house and farm, and now I'm glad when I have bread and beer."

The farmer went onto the front lawn and sat on a stunted tree. It was a cold and clear star-filled night, but Wulf didn't notice the chill. He quietly ate his bread and sausage as always, drank his schnapps, and pondered his course of action. He sat there until dawn, when sounds stirred again from inside the house. The serving girl, who was fetching water from the farm, called to him to come have a bowl of soup, which he then did.

The baggage attendant also came into the house. Harm got news from him as to where the train was headed. Also, that the man who slapped him was a devil incarnate, a true abuser of mankind. "He can stand by and be entertained as a girl is tortured to death!" said the servant. He told of further blood-curdling things, which gave Harm hot and cold chills down his spine.

After the man left, Wulf-farmer put on his dumbest peasant face and wandered about to and fro, as if he didn't know what to do with himself from boredom. There was a powder horn and bullet sack lying on the window sill; when no one was watching, he threw both over the fence, under an elderberry bush. Then he looked around until he found a rifle, which he likewise acquired and put off to the side.

Finally he met up with the young officer who was with him at his farm; Wulf asked him when he could have his horses back. The young man, who had drunk too much the night before and gambled away all his money, shrugged his shoulders and walked past without a word. When Harm followed him and said: "But you made me a promise!" he turned and shouted: "Haven't you had enough yet? Goto the Devil!"

"If not, then not!" murmured the farmer. He let himself be served another plate of bread soup and a piece of dry bread, as the innkeeper said: "The swine who took your money drank it up here!"

When the coast was clear, he pocketed the powder horn and bullet sack and put the rifle under his coat, looking around to make sure no one noticed. He then ducked from one tree to another, until he was far enough from the pub and well into the moors.

He was very calm, for he knew how he intended to get paid. He went very slowly in a large circle around the break towards the main road, always keeping himself under cover. He sought a position near a large patch of peat through which no rider could penetrate, and there he waited for his moment.

He heard a shot fired in the distance from across the moors. A black cock crowed from the bogs; a fox crossed over the road diagonally, got wind of the farmer, then turned back; juniper thrushes landed in the field; mice peeped in the elderberry bushes; a magpie flew past overhead.

Then a horn sounded in the town, once . . . twice . . . and a third time. "Now . . . now!" thought Harm. It was not long before he heard the racket of the wagons, the crack of whips, and the whinny of a horse . . . a mare. One stallion answered back, and then all others. The trumpeter blew a lively piece and the riders sang along; it actually sounded good. Wulf recognized the song and whistled quietly to himself, laughing and thinking "Soon . . . soon!"

They approached: one . . . two . . . three riders . . . then a whole bunch more. Then another, the trumpeter. Then the standard bearer, a fat man with a jolly face. Then the young officer, and next to him another. They were talking to each other, then laughed loudly; one of them pointed to a raven that flew over the road and suddenly sheered to the left. Then a lady came riding by with an attendant on either side. She was the one who accompanied the colonel, an exceptionally beautiful girl. She turned around and called to someone behind her.

And then came the colonel. He appeared to have drunk little and gotten a good night's rest. He was tapping his dapple-gray's neck with his right hand, the one which held those yellow gauntlets.

Wulf took a good look at the man, for he wanted to remember that face always. Then he put the man in his front sight. At that very moment the colonel turned full-face towards his direction. First he aimed at the chest, but then he placed the sight a bit lower; as the shot rang out, he saw through the muzzle flash that the man threw both arms into the air and tipped off to the side. Right after that he heard him cry out: "Oh, Jesus!" followed by the scream of the lady.

But by then the farmer had already gone a stretch further. He had planned out ahead of time exactly how to retreat so that no one would see him. As the hue and cry arose, and a dozen shots were fired into the elderberry bush where he had been lying in wait, Wulf already had the peat pit and a deep marsh behind him. He crawled from one birch shrub to another, until he reached a hillock from which he could see as far as the road.

He had to chuckle, how they rode hither and yon and amidst one another, almost as if it were recreational sport! And now he laughed out loud, for three . . . no, four riders who had rushed into the marshes suddenly disappeared behind a great splash of water.

"A bit too cold this morning for a swim!" Wulf mused, and shook his head as another three horsemen rode into the break. Two sank immediately and fell over. However the other, who was riding a dappled, almost reached the heath. But there the horse broke through, the rider hit the morass with a squelch, and the horse galloped further, without its master.

Wulf sprang up and crept along, hunched down, from one juniper bush to another until he was far enough away. He saw that several other riders dismounted and went into the break on foot. He then ran, as well as he could, to where the dappled was trotting back and forth. The animal didn't know what to do to get out of the morass. When it saw the farmer, it snorted in a friendly manner. Harm was able to leisurely take it in hand and tie it to one of the bushes.

The farmer stayed in hiding behind a juniper long enough until the train was again underway. He could estimate the number of horses. The dappled-gray went on unmanned, and the lady was no longer riding out in the open. That outlandish red hat she was wearing could now be spotted on one of the wagons.

The farmer nodded to himself, for he had accomplished his mission. He waited long enough for the train to disappear into the woods, and then a quarter of an hour longer.

Then he carefully went to the place where he had hidden the rifle, reloaded it, and crept over to where the horseman had fallen so severely. He soon found the soldier. The man's head was on his chest and he moved no more; he had broken his neck.

This was no lowly trooper, rather a sergeant. Wulf grabbed him by the belt, cut open his jacket, and then laughed to himself: eleven ducats[29] were sewn into the lining on the back, and seven more on the chest. There were three thalers in his pocket and even more schillings. Additionally, he had a very fine dagger, along with the saber on his belt. Harm took the knife, left the saber, but kept the two long pistols that he found in the horse's saddlebag.

He was completely satisfied after also finding white bread, a bottle of schnapps, a fried chicken, and salt in another pouch. He sat next to the horse and quietly had breakfast, giving the bread that he had taken with him from Bissendorf to the dapple. He then filled his pipe, smoked it leisurely to the end, and then headed towards home at a lively pace.

From a distance, he could already see that his wife was looking for him. She laughed and cried intermittently as she

29. Ducat, any of several various gold coins formerly used throughout Europe.

spotted him. "Oh, God! Harm!" she sobbed. "I didn't get a wink of sleep all night! God be praised and thanked that you have returned. I was so afraid! But where did you get that dapple? And where are our horses?"

Her husband laughed cheerfully: "Yes, girl, I had to leave them behind. But I was handsomely paid! Look here!" He showed her the money. "But now I'm hungry like a wolf . . . haven't had such an appetite in a long while. Yesterday I didn't eat properly, due to aggravation. How's the boy? And did anything else happen?"

He was so lively and had such bright eyes that his wife was amazed. The fear that she had known the day and night before changed into pure joy. A day like this had not been seen on the farm in a long time, so much laughter and whistling were heard! Harm gave his boy a piggy-back, let him ride on his knees, and sang for him the song that the trumpeter had blown that morning.

A rider approached the farm: it was Drewes. "Did you hear the latest?" he quietly asked Wulf, sniggering like an executioner. "This morning the Weimaraner colonel . . . or whatever rank he was . . . was shot to death from the bushes behind Bissendorf . . . near the old wolf pits. That is, he didn't die right away. He got as far as Hope and there his breath left him. I heard the story in Mellendorf. Also, a sergeant and another rider drowned in the break when they went looking for the sharpshooter. Those dunces! They should've stayed out of the marshes!"

He looked sideways at farmer Wulf: "You've lost your horses, I heard. One of your field hands mentioned that you were paid well for them, though. That's a real wonder! They took two right off of my plow without so much as a 'God Bless!' in return. Nice weather today . . . but I think it'll change by tonight. Well, adieu!"

He acted as if he were departing, but then turned around once more: "Well . . . are you still disgusted with me over that time I soiled my walking stick with blood? That's okay . . . don't answer . . . and I won't mention it again either! Done is done. We're not the kind of people who ask for anything or give anything away. Just so you know . . . day after tomorrow we're going to talk about how things will go around here from now on. One for all and all for one . . . that's how it's got to be . . . otherwise we'll all . . . to a man . . . wind up going to the dogs. In Wettmar the hellions violently raped two farmers' daughters . . . and in Berghof they beat a landowner so bad that he died. Because of these things we're going to meet up on the Hingst mountain, day after tomorrow . . . around nine. One or two men from each town around the break. You have to represent Ödringen . . . the Burvogt is down with his bad cough again."

"Oh, I also wanted to say . . . those firebrands that were hanging around Bissendorf yesterday . . . they won't come back here. They're glad to move on elsewhere . . . word is that the papist General Till . . . or whatever he's called . . . is on their trail. Let's hope that he doesn't pass this way. Adders and vipers are two different species, but both are poisonous."

He again looked sideways at Harm: "But don't worry about regretting your business with them . . . or that you'll have to return the money and dapple you received. However, that horse looks outlandish . . . I'd color it up a bit . . . otherwise people will laugh at you when you're at the plow, saying: 'Oh, that Wulf-farmer! Now he plows with a black-spotted cow!' Well, then . . . until day after tomorrow!"

And with that he left. Harm took Drewes' advice, and by evening the dapple was a black horse. He had barely finished the job when the Engenser showed up again. "Man," he said, "you've got to help! News has just come from Wiekenberg that thirty men are moving through the moors. They burned a farmhouse in Wiekenberg and beat the people there, leaving them lame and crippled . . . so we're gathering fifty or sixty together. Up now! Onwards, to the merry hunt!"

Wulf made a morose face. He had hoped to get a good night's sleep, and now he was going to have to slog around the moors like a wolf, lying in the bushes all night again. And then there was his wife . . . she hadn't been so cheerful in such a long time. Her eyes were so merry when she looked at him, and she again had color in her cheeks, like in the days before misfortune struck. On top of that, who knows where the men that Drewes mentioned were headed? Finally, they hadn't done him any harm. The business with the colonel . . . that was another matter . . . he had slugged him in the face! But to hunt down and ambush people with whom he had no prior dealings? This didn't sit well with Harm.

"You know something, Drewes," he said; "I can barely hold my head up. I was out in the open all last night, and then spent most of the day over the moors and heath. And my wife . . . you know how she is! For the first time she seems like her old self. I can't leave her today . . . I had enough worries about her this whole year. And my being there tonight won't make the porridge any thicker . . . especially since I have no reliable horse. So keep me out of it . . . at least for today."

The Engenser looked at him with an appraising eye. "That's true . . . you look like your head is hanging in the direction of the bed. Well, we'll finish with them either way. Maybe you can come early tomorrow morning. We're leaving soon so that we can take them to task before the early dawn. But then next time we'll be counting on you! Consider this . . . if you don't want to help us, do you think that anyone else is going to lift a finger for you? You've already experienced enough to know better than waiting until someone again does something to you before you strike back. Dead foxes bite no more! But as you wish. And so, adieu!"

Harm's heart lightened thoroughly when Drewes rode away. As he went into the house, he whistled that song to himself, the one that the horsemen had sung this morning:

"Nothing more beautiful can delight me
Than when the summer approaches . . .
The roses bloom in the garden,
Ah yes, in the garden,
And trumpeters blow in the field!"

~

CHAPTER 5

The Marauders

It was no mean hunt that the farmers made. As the fog lifted, they saw the gang approaching. They waited until they had them in the middle of the marshy break, and then shot them down like corralled deer; not one survived. There were twenty-two that lay there, old men with faces like leather and young lads with milk-white and rosy complexions. One of them (whom Drewes had overtaken) had cried out: "Mercy! My Mother!" But that didn't help him. The Engenser responded: "Young wildcats have claws too!" and struck him dead.

He chuckled as he related it all to Wulf, as if it had been nothing more than sport, and his large white teeth shimmered. "This time it was a success!" he grinned. "And the work was not without profit!" he added. "My share alone was eleven solid thalers. Too bad they weren't horsemen. Acquiring a few horses cheaply would have suited me. But now I have to head home, otherwise I'll hear it from the wife." He shrugged and Harm laughed, for he knew of Christel Drewes' sharp tongue, against which few could contend.

Rose called Harm to dinner. His heart leapt in his chest when he saw her! Life was beautiful, all things considered. Peace would surely come again. The aristocrats must certainly rue playing these war games which cost an ungodly amount of money and men. And what one heard by the by was just too dreadful: everywhere Murder, Arson, Pestilence and Famine. Life in the break was certainly better than elsewhere. War is war, and feathers fly when geese are plucked; no way around it.

Thus thought the farmer, as he took joy in his pretty wife and the boy who grew cuter by the moment, and who could say a few more words with the passing of each day. Wulf mused: "If another child arrives to occupy Rose, then she'll totally recover from all that happened before." And indeed, it was so. A small girl arrived, a strong and healthy child, and the wife returned to her former self.

The war was certainly far from over, but on the Wulfstead one hardly noticed it. Now and again a troop would move through the land, sometimes of this sort, sometimes of that sort; wherever they walked, the path was no longer clean. More than once smoke was seen during the day, and by evening a red glow shone over the moors.

Hither and yon there also appeared gangs of marauders and partisan followers; but they watched their step, for the moors were gaining infamy in the eyes of all vagabonds. Some went into the marshes, but fewer came out; for Drewes had organized a proper scouting network, and no sooner would the horn sound than the farmers would band together, and Good Lord, how they hunted!

The moorland could tell some harsh tales . . . but it remained silent.

Silent, that is, but for the warning signs that the gypsies carved into the tallest, most noticeable trees, and all other landmarks. Silent, except for the many shiny gold pieces and many solid thalers now in the farmers' strongboxes, the many horses standing in their stalls, and the pistols, lances, shotguns, sabers and daggers hanging in all dens. All these things told of the men who once owned them, and over whose bones now moor sod lays and weeds grow.

For several years the farmers pursued this business quietly; all men knew of it, but no one discussed it. Drewes ruled with an iron hand. It was said that a hired hand, Metjen from Ehlershausen, stood in suspicion of dealing with some of Tilly's[30] soldiers, betraying to them paths and directions through the moors. Three days later, by the hand of Drewes and two other farmers, he was found hung from an apple tree in front of his house, a noose of thin willow limbs around the neck.

One gorgeous early autumn day the Wulf-farmer got a message to be at Hingst mountain by four o'clock. The triple tax levy, affecting landowners and laborers alike, was to be discussed, or so he was told.

It was so warm that the sweat ran openly from under his hat as he rode through the moors. An eagle circled overhead in the blue heavens, sometimes looking like silver, sometimes like gold. Here and there the heathland was still blooming and flocks of small chirping birds flew continuously over the break.

Harm took a deep breath, and as he rode he whistled his favorite song lightly and thought: "By eight, when the children go to bed, I'll be home again." He enjoyed thinking about that, how they giggled and squealed when he tickled them!

About a hundred farmers were gathered on Hingst mountain. They stood in small groups around the old heathen ruins and spoke of the weather and livestock, or sat on the

---

30. Johan Tzerclaes, Count of Tilly (1559-1632), General of The Catholic League armies that put down the Bohemian Protestant rebellion at White Mountain (1620). After numerous other victories during the decade of the 1620's, he was given chief command of all Imperial forces. He was defeated by Gustavus Adolphus and the Swedish forces at Breitenfeld (1631) and again at Lech (1632), where he was fatally wounded.

ground and supped or smoked. Drewes made himself comfortable on a large boulder. He held his pipe between his teeth and carved notches in his blackthorn walking stick in such an exacting manner that one appeared identical to the next. When he saw the Ödringer ride up, he nodded to him. "Fine second crop weather today!" he remarked. "Actually too nice to waste in gabbing . . . but talk we must, for there are important matters at hand."

After a quarter of an hour had passed, he told the farmhand by his side: "Now everyone is surely here . . . sound off!" At that the boy blew his horn three times. Everyone stopped talking or eating and gathered around the old pagan altar upon which Drewes stood. He knocked his stick against the boulder and looked over the crowd until everyone was quiet.

He began: "Dear friends . . . Today I have something to say to you all that you'll find easy to swallow. We've had hard years behind us, and who knows what is yet to come? It seems as if our Lord God has abandoned his dominion, and now Satan incarnate has taken the reins in hand. Here in the break, things have been somewhat tolerable. One or the other of us has certainly lost some hair . . . some even a piece of skin and possibly flesh and blood. But in other areas it has been truly gruesome. Whatever's left of the Mansfelders, or the Braunschweigers . . . who got their just reward in Westphalia when Till...or whatever he's called . . . reeled them in soundly,[31] so that most of them drank their own blood . . . where was I? Ah, so . . . whether Imperial troops, or Papists,[32] or

31. Battle of Stadtlohn (August 9, 1623), Tilly routed the forces of Duke Christian Of Braunshweig, which for all intents marked the latter stage of the so-called Palatinate phase of the Thirty Years War, wherein Mansfeld disbanded his forces (though he would return later) and Duke Christian's military career ended.

32. Troops loyal to the Pope (or at least the concept of the Papacy being the ultimate authority over Catholic nations and peoples).

Leaguers[33] . . . they have all the same maliciousness. Women and children are not safe from those dogs!"

He looked from man to man: "Each man, no matter how poor, holds his wife and children dear to his heart . . . and is devoted to home and farm. Let us protect all of those, like we've done thus far . . . to the extent that we've been able." (With that he pointed towards the marshes and grinned broadly, and all the men laughed quietly). "Up until now, we've had to defend ourselves in secret when we wished to rid ourselves of the highwaymen who loitered around, or the rabble that traipsed about. Afterwards . . . we couldn't look each other in the eye. But from now on, that's changed!"

He lifted his staff high and showed the notches: "Look here! I have one hundred and seventeen notches carved here . . . thirty-two on one side . . . the rest on the other. The eighty-five notches signify the vagabonds, sneak thieves, gypsies, brigands and one traitorous dog that I've assisted in delivering to where they belong, according to God and justice . . . namely, under the earth for the worms to eat . . . that is, if they're not too disgusted."

"The thirty-two notches, however . . . my friends, they signify the people of this sort that I killed with my own hands."

He took a deep breath, wiped his forehead, and spoke in a more subdued tone: "Our Lord God will forgive me. Eye for eye, tooth for tooth . . . thus saith the Scriptures. We are not robbers and murderers! But when the wolf goes after our grazing livestock . . . or the marten goes after our chickens . . . then we act quickly and don't waste time thinking. Up until the day that the oppression started around here, I hadn't given a blow to anyone since my days as a child in short pants.

---

33. The Catholic League, an alliance (1609–35) of Catholic powers in Germany, led by Maximillian I, Duke of Bavaria, in order to thwart the spread of Protestantism. The armies in the field were commanded by Tilly.

And I would have preferred to keep my hands clean! But what is necessary is necessary . . . I sleep as soundly as always . . . I don't think there are any of us here that feel differently."

He looked at the row of men and winked at one or the other who were watching him with clear eyes. "One thing, though, my dear friends," he continued his speech; "It has nevertheless bothered us. What we did had to be done . . . but it wasn't our intention to do it without the permission of our Lord Duke." (He removed his hat, and the others did likewise). He then spoke in a brighter tone, laughing: "But from today on, things are different! For our Lord Duke . . . may God protect him . . . has given word that we are to see to it that we defend ourselves to the best of our ability . . . and all rotten curs who don't belong here are to be shot dead like mad dogs!"

He laughed so that his large teeth were visible: "Well, let us not disappoint the will of our duke! Of course we'd prefer to live like before . . . working in peace and praising God. But for now things are otherwise . . . therefore I say to each of you: whatever doesn't belong here . . . whatever is traipsing through the countryside robbing and stealing . . . oppressing people and burning houses . . . that is lawless trash . . . and must be handled as such! Curse for curse, blow for blow, blood for blood! On this let us hold fast . . . so that we and our kind prosper and live long on the earth!"

He wiped the sweat from his brow and closed with: "So . . . now you know how things stand. And I believe, my dear friends, that it's only right when I ask you to follow my lead."

With that, he took off his hat and raised it high as he shouted: "Long live Duke Christian, our most gracious lord!"

The crows flying over the break suddenly sheered off to the side, startled by the shouting of the men. All had shining eyes as they approached Drewes and remarked: "Drew-boy, that was some talk! The preacher couldn't have done it better!"

But then they listened soberly again as the Wiekenbergers mentioned how everywhere was crawling with soldiers: Danes, Leaguers[34], Mansfelders, and Braunschweigers . . . who Tilly and Wallenstein[35] chased back and forth like dogs on hens . . . and who were committing arson and murder worse than before.

No one knew for sure exactly what was happening. One said: "The Danes are trying to take over the country!"; others remarked: "No, it's about eradicating the new faith and making us all Catholics again!" Still others reckoned that the Emperor had washed his hands of the whole thing and now visits with the Devil for tea and conversation, while Wallenstein and Tilly are only trying to enrich themselves on land and cash . . . that's the driving force behind it all!

The Wulf-farmer found Drewes' speech to be outstanding and correct on all accounts, though his attention had been divided; he thought more about his wife and children, and how it was about time for him to ride home, lest he miss putting the little mites to bed. He chuckled as he remembered how Hermke had pulled on his ears this afternoon, so hard that it smarted!

He rode home with Klaus Hennecke, the son of the town's current Burvogt. The air was warm and mellow; the peewits

34. League Of The Hague, the 1625 Protestant alliance of Dutch, English, and Danes whose soldiers fought under Christian IV, who was both King of Denmark and Duke Of Holstein.

35. Albrecht von Wallenstein (1583–1634) commander of the Imperial armies who allied with Tilly and dealt many defeats to Protestant forces between 1625 and 1627, most notably finishing off Mansfeld at Dessau and Silesia. Fearing his growing power and influence, the Emperor Ferdinand II dismissed him in 1630, whereupon Tilly took over command of his forces. He was recalled in 1632 in an effort to stop Gustavus Adolphus; after a few minor successes, the Imperials were defeated at the Battle Of Lützen. In 1634 he was again dismissed and charged with treason, then assassinated by his senior officers, probably at the behest of the emperor.

called from the ground, and the plovers answered from the skies.

Klaus finally spoke: "Our father's condition is steadily getting worse . . . he's been in bed for eight weeks already. I think this time he won't pull through." He gazed out over the moorland, then said: "Look . . . what sort of strange fancy cloud is that over Ödringen? Eh . . . that looks a lot like smoke . . . but it's surely only a cloud."

That was Harm's opinion as well. As they circled the peat bogs and faced the wind, their horses snorted as one and appeared skittish, so that both farmers reckoned they scented a wolf. But when they rode a stretch further, Hennecke stopped and sniffed, then said: "That smells sure enough like smoke! Those rascal cowherd boys are probably up to their mischief again." Harm reckoned he was right, for it did smell like smoke; but he thought nothing further of it.

Finally they smelled nothing, as the wind changed direction through the woods. But when they got to the high heath the smell was again strong. When they had the winding paths behind them, and were atop the hill, they both cried as one: "Oh God!" There, where Ödringen lay, the air was all black.

They looked at each other; one appeared as sallow as the other. Without a word they set their horses to a gallop. The burning smell grew ever worse, and what weighed on their hearts even heavier was that the haystacks on the meadows lay exactly as they had when they rode out that afternoon. They pushed the horses for all they were worth. As they came out of the woods, they stopped and shuddered throughout their whole bodies; on the path before them lay the cowherd, dead on his back, his dog sniffing all around him.

They dismounted and looked closely at Tonnes. His throat had been cut. They pulled him to the side and then listened towards the town. It was very still, the only sound being the caws of the jackdaws over the oaks. They went closer, step by step . . . one hand on a dagger, the other on the reins. In the path lay a broken stoneware bottle, of a sort that no one in the town possessed. Further on they found a bloody cloth, and next to it a piece of sausage. They stopped and listened, but nothing could be heard; no people's voices were noticeable, not one cow lowed, no hen cackled, no hound barked.

They came to the Reinkenstead. It still stood, but the windows were broken in, the doors open, and bedcovers lay strewn about, along with straw and hay and oats. Everything in the house was broken and scattered. At the end of the hallway, a tabby cat was walking around and caterwauling. The living room looked like a pig sty, full of garbage. No stool was whole, no dish unbroken. On the front lawn lay the head, legs, and intestines of a red spotted calf; next to it, a spinning wheel in several pieces.

Klaus and Harm said nothing. Next they came to Hingstmann's farm. There it looked exactly the same, except that across the vestibule lay a dead herdsboy. He had a deep hole in his forehead.

By Mertens it was no different, and the same over at the Henkenstead, except at least there were no bodies to be found there. All the other farms were plundered and had everything broken in two, but the farmers appeared to have gotten wind in time and were able to escape and hide.

Suddenly, Harm looked around wildly and called: "Yes, but where is it burning now, then? Holy God!" He mounted and rushed away, with Klaus Hennecke close at his heels. They rode straight across the heathland, and the further they went, the more it smelled like smoke. Then Harm stopped and dismounted. His face looked as if he were about to cry as he stared at the spot where his farmhouse used to be. It was now engulfed in haze and dense smoke, with a flame visible here and there.

"Wha-wha-what is th-th-this then?" he stuttered. His legs nearly buckled under him and Klaus had to grab him by the arm. Then he screamed: "Rose . . . Ro-ose!" He ran around the burning site, into the backyard, looked into the drawing well, climbed around the burning joists, looked upwards, shook his head and said with a laugh that made Hennecke's blood run cold: "In the fort . . . they're probably in the fortress in the break!"

Klaus nodded: "Yes, I think so too. They probably all went together along with the livestock. And Hingstmann's boy and Tonnes . . . they were caught alone and unawares outside . . . that's why they met their fate. Let's get to the walled fort.... and if they're not there, then we've got to . . . yes . . . it's best, we'll ride first to Engensen . . . we'll get the news from the Drewes farm first."

They mounted and rode over the heath through the pines, and from there into the break. The twilight was falling as they arrived. An owl flew overhead and screeched weakly when it reached the woods. Fog rose thickly behind the peat bogs, ducks beat into the air, and deer startled in the meadows.

No one spoke. Now and again they'd stop to listen in the direction of where the old embankment lay, and then they'd start along the trail again, where one could tell people and livestock had recently passed.

The forest was so dark that they had to dismount. The path zig-zagged in sudden turns, sometimes right, sometimes straight, then partially left and so on. Now and again a dove would sound to the fore, or some animal would rush through the woods. The two men would stand still and listen from time to time, but never heard any human voices or animals lowing.

Finally, it seemed like they spotted a light ahead. They stopped and heard some beast bellowing across the way. Then the cock of a rifle clicked, followed by another, and a voice that sounded like young Bolle called out quietly: "Who's there?" Harm whispered back: "It's us, Harm and Klaus. Where's my wife?"

Adolf Bolle choked, as if he had something caught in his throat, then grumbled: "First come on into the fort! I'm on guard duty and don't know who all is here. It was head over heels today, because we had to rush madly so that the rabble didn't latch onto us. But Ul-father . . . I saw him earlier . . . before I took my post."

"What was that, then?!" Wulf startled, as something black bounded by in front of him. It was his dog. It acted as if crazy, barking and yowling in turns; then it jumped up high on the farmer, licked his hands, ran away and barked, then returned and suddenly sat down, crying so terribly that Bolle grumbled "Quiet, boy!"

As Wulf entered the wall, the first person he saw was Reinken's wife. As she came face to face with him she cried out: "Oh, God . . . Wulf-fellow!" and started to weep. "What's wrong?!" pleaded Harm. "Where's Rose?!" But the woman was sobbing so hard that it made her recoil, and she couldn't say a word.

Harm looked around, but whenever he caught someone's eye they quickly looked away and retreated. Finally he found his father-in-law. "Where's Rose?" he barely managed to get out, being very hoarse from fear. The old man had an expression on his face as if he had been pulled from the grave. "Yes, boy," he said as he reached for both of Harm's hands, "Yes, boy . . . our Rose is with the Lord God!" He then started to weep bitterly.

Harm made a motion as if he wanted to throttle him: "What's that you say?! Dead?!" He started to laugh. "That's just . . . that can't . . . speak up, man . . . no one will tell me where Rose is!" And then he called out in a voice that sounded as if it would break down the fortress wall: "Rose?!!! Rose?!!! Where are you?!!!"

Hingstmann ran to his side: "Quiet, man . . . father Rennecken lay dying, and Horstmann's woman has come down with something from all the agitation and isn't doing well." He offered him his flask: "Drink something now." But Wulf pushed him away: "I want to know what's happened to my wife . . . I want to know! And where are the children?! My Hemmke and the little girl?! Dear folks, somebody say something already!"

Two more farmers came up: "Well . . . he's got to know eventually," said Mertens. He put his hand on Wulf's shoulders: "Yes, Harm, what's the use? Your beloved wife is gone . . . she stayed in the house. And the kids too. And your father . . . also one of the farmhands and the two maids. The Devil knows how on earth those beastly curs found their way to your house, which lay off so remotely!"

Harm looked from one to the other. He seemed like a child who didn't dare to move, as if standing before a dog he didn't trust. His rubbed his hands up and down his clothes, his lips trembled, and a cold sweat broke from his forehead. Anyone could hear how his heart labored within his chest and how his breath could barely clear his throat. Finally he agonized: "Well, were they burned . . . or what happened?"

The men looked away. Finally Horstmann said: "We don't know anything more about it. The only person who survived is your farmhand, Thedel. But he's just about out of his mind . . . he's sitting back there by the fire . . . sneering and constantly staring at that knife which he holds in his hand."

Harm stumbled and rushed to where he saw the lad sitting. As he stood before him, the young man laughed at him and held up the knife; but then he suddenly let it drop, hit both hands against his head, and wept openly. The farmer shook him "Boy! Tell me, then . . . what exactly happened?

Not one person wants to tell me anything about it!" He sat down next to him and put his hand on the back of his neck: "Talk!" he ordered.

The lad looked at him earnestly, as if he had never laid eyes on him before; then he began: "They're all dead . . . all of them together. The mistress is dead . . . Hinnerk is dead . . . Hermke and the little girl. Also Trina is dead . . . and the grandfather and my sister Alheid . . . also dead. All of them dead . . . except me. I was off in the forest . . . chopping wood . . . and heard nothing until the beatings started . . . when it was already too late . . . they came out of the break."

He couldn't say too much, since most of it was over when he got back. But what little he did see was such that it made him pull away from the farmer, whose face grew dark and whose eyes gave him a chill down his spine. But the farmer said: "Continue, boy, continue . . . I must know everything!" Now and then the farmer groaned or chattered with his mouth, so that Thedel could hear his teeth rattle.

When Wulf had gotten everything out of the lad, he said: "Yes, Thedel . . . me and you . . . that's all that remains of the Wulfstead. What do you want to do now? You want to find work elsewhere . . . or stay with me? Understand me rightly . . . I can't play the farmer anymore! Where the Devil has harvested, I no longer have the will to plow and sow." He sat down for a short moment, then said: "But in what direction did the murderers head?"

The young one shrugged his shoulders: "They went straight across the heath and split up by the big shade pine. The gypsies headed towards Berghof . . . the others probably headed towards Celle . . . at least that's where the man told me they intended to go."

"Man? What man?!" interrupted the farmer. The lad laughed diabolically: "The one who got so drunk on your honey beer that he couldn't move, and so he laid down and fell asleep in the field."

"Well, where is he now?" continued Harm. "He's surely still laying there," grinned the lad. "How so, still there?" asked the farmer. The lad laughed openly across his entire face: "Well . . . because I bound his hands and feet as he lay there like a barrel . . . also, because he . . . once he stirred and I got out of him what I wanted to know . . . didn't have much life left in him."

The farmer laughed darkly: "What did you do, Thedel?" And his grim laughter grew hardier when the lad showed him the knife and told him what he had done to the man. "For he was the worst of the lot!" said the lad. "He was the one who killed . . . my sister. Him and that Holy Cross and Suckling. And they've got to answer for it too, before I can rest peacefully in my grave!"

The farmer looked at him dumbly: "Holy Cross? Suckling? What's all that mean?" Thedel said: "When it was almost over, and most of them were drunk like swine, I crawled behind the haystacks. From there I saw a man . . . taller than any man I've ever seen . . . but he had a very small head . . . like a child . . . with a voice to match . . . when he opened his mouth . . . and also no beard. They called him 'Suckling'. And the other one . . . he was as short and fat as a cabbage barrel . . . with a ginger-colored twisted moustache . . . and two scars on his face . . . each thick as a finger and red like a cock's comb . . . one from the forehead to the mouth . . . the other from one ear to the other . . . so that they formed a cross . . . and that's surely why they teased him with the name 'Holy Cross.'"

He stared out before him: "Those two murdered my sister . . . I heard them make jokes about it . . . those two and the other . . . the drunk who remained lying in the field. Well, him I took care of! I stuffed his mouth with rags . . . I thought that if he started to bellow . . . and the others heard . . . then I'd be the one caught with my pants down. The other two whistled after him for awhile . . . then they got bored and moved on. I'm now curious to see if he'll live until morning!"

In the middle of talking he fell asleep. The farmer put a coat over him and noticed that the lad slept as soundly as always. The farmer often glanced over to him; he looked like a child who couldn't harm a fly. He was the only person in the whole town who couldn't watch a pig being slaughtered, yet he had flayed that marauder wide open, like an executioner's lackey torturing a wretched criminal.

"He did right!" thought the farmer. "Drewes had said: 'Curse for curse, blow for blow, blood for blood'!" Wulf looked into the fire and saw therein a tall man with a small head and thin voice, and another, short and fat like a keg, with two scars crossing on his face. He saw them spread out before him with bound hands and old rags in their mouths, the sweat of fear on their foreheads. He stood before them, kicking them with his foot as he held his knife before their eyes.

He sat there for a long time and thought of nothing else. But suddenly his eyes grew moist. In one of the sod huts an infant was crying and a woman sang:

> "Lullaby Lea,
> Can't you sleep here by me?
> Let's try something different, maybe
> A bed in the meadows for my baby,
> Lullaby Lea."

CHAPTER 6

~

The Moorland Farmers

It was broad daylight when Harm Wulf awoke. He had fallen asleep while sitting, and had slept so deeply that he wasn't fully awake at first, and looked around wildly, not sure of where he was.

But then he stood up, slowly and heavily, as if he had not twenty-four, but forty-eight years behind him. Hingstmann (who had just passed by) startled when he saw him, for Wulf-farmer had the face of an old man and eyes in which little life shone; the sides of his hair had turned grey.

"If only he could cry, Ul-father!" said Reinke's wife. "It's so frightening, how this is eating the man up inside!" But Harm didn't cry. He ate, as always, but said little beyond 'yes' and 'no' as he helped make the entrenchments higher and built sheds and did whatever other work was needed.

At ten o'clock he went out with Thedel. When they returned, both had a gleam in their eye, and the lad grinned so incessantly that it was dreadful to behold.

"What are you going to do now, Harm?" his father-in-law asked that evening as they sat around the fire. "Do you want to rebuild the farm?" His son-in-law shook his head: "I have other work in mind."

"It might be that I'll be gone for awhile . . . or maybe I'll return soon. Just so you know . . . those vultures didn't find the money. I would gladly have given it to them . . . had everything else remained as it was. If you find yourself in dire straits, you know where to find it . . . it's no small amount. And in the other place . . . you know what I'm talking about . . . there is enough seed corn . . . also, a large amount of sausage and ham and cheese . . . mead as well . . . pistols and a rifle, too. Can you spare some tobacco?"

He filled his pipe, held a small branch to the fire until it caught on, and lit his tobacco with it. "You know something?" he then continued. "This is how things stand with me . . . I don't have a lust for life anymore . . . let me finish! Maybe it will return when I settle accounts with those two arsonists . . . that's what I'm set on. Whoever spills the blood of others, his blood should likewise be spilled. Thedel wants to come with . . . they stick in his craw just as much as mine . . . on account of Alheid. Gripper can stay with you . . . the dog would only get in my way."

A large flock of birds approached, then landed in the high trees and squawked noisily. Harm looked up: "There's that nonsense again! Hingstmann's father said they were an omen of war and plague. Maybe he's right . . . I've never seen such birds in my time. I found one dead on the ground in the heath . . . it was red like blood . . . with a beak that criss-crossed. Anyway, what are all of you here now going to do? In Ödringen your lives aren't safe on any given day . . . what happened yesterday can repeat tomorrow . . . I think it will be best to hunker down right here and build in the moors . . . on Peerhobst Hill. You won't easily be found . . . and enough fruit grows there for times of need. The fort here has to be made more secure . . . the trenches need to be dug deeper . . . and a wolf pit made near every turn of the access paths."

The old man nodded: "Yes, yesterday we ourselves said likewise. We have enough livestock and horses . . . and the best thing to do while war still wages is for all of us to eat out of one pot . . . so to speak . . . regardless of the annoyance. But then you should stay too! What do you want out there in the wide world? Look here, son . . . misfortune has struck . . . and it weighs on me as much as you. You'll find another wife eventually, but . . . I have no daughter. You have your whole life ahead of you . . . with me, it's another story. Nevertheless, I'm staying here . . . where I were born."

The other shook his head. "I'll come back when I'm able. But I swore an oath to myself and I have to stick by it. All the more because I would go crazy here . . . remembering how things used to be . . . with every step I take." He called to his man Thedel: "Show me your knife!" The lad grinned and took it out of the sheath. "That's good! Get some sleep now . . . we want to get an early start in the morning!"

He looked at Ul: "The man who killed Alheid is dead. Thedel saw to that . . . along with the wolves. We buried him this morning under the broad pines behind my farm . . . there are all kinds of stones on the spot. But two of the miscreants still live . . . an inhumanly tall man with white hair . . . but still young . . . with an unusually small head and a voice like a child . . . and then another . . . short and fat like a barrel . . . with a ginger twisted moustache and two scars on his face . . . each thick as a finger and bright red . . . one from forehead to mouth and the other across the ears . . . so that it looks like a cross . . . therefore they call him the "Holy Cross" . . . and the other "Suckling". If they show their faces around here you are not to kill them . . . I want them alive, you hear? I'll be checking back from time to time."

~

It was well into fall, however, before he returned. Bernd Bolles, who had guard duty that day on the Halloberg outpost hills, had just remarked to Gerd Mertens, who was keeping him company: "How nice the bare birch trees look . . . like pure gold!" Then he stretched his neck like a black rooster and nudged Gerd in the ribs: "What's that over there in the bulrushes? It looks like a horse and rider . . . sure enough it absolutely is . . . two, as a matter of fact!"

He ducked behind the bushes and waved to Gerd. When the riders got as far as the thick pines, he put his long horn to his lips and blew loudly so that a hare which was sleeping under a heath shrub shot out wildly and ran along the foot path. Three times the youth sounded the horn, each time a different sound. After a pause, he blew a fourth time, so loud and long that it could be heard for a half-mile radius.

"They're on their guard!" said Harm Wulf to Thedel. "We'll have to identify ourselves so that we don't get a rib-full of buckshot before they recognize us. Show them how you can play!" The sidekick took the small horn that hung on his saddle, wiped his lips, cleared his throat, spat, and then blew in the direction of the Halloberg. From the hills came a short reply, and Thedel answered in kind.

"That sounds exactly like Thedel Niehus, that bugler there!" said Bernd. "But what sort of clothes is he wearing? He looks more like an actual soldier! What do you make of it?" The other put his hand above his eyes as he looked from behind the shrubs: "Yep, that's him . . . for sure. And the other . . . that's Wulf-fellow. I almost didn't recognize him . . . he's grown such a beard! Well, let me sound the reply."

He again raised his horn, but the other stopped him: "Wait a moment!" They stayed under cover until the riders were very close. Then he came forward and called: "Well . . . back from your travels, Harm? You too, Thedel? We almost didn't recognize you, the way you now look. Okay now, Gerd . . . sound off!" he called to the lad who stood partially to the side, laughing broadly, for Thedel was his good friend, and farmer Wulf once saved his life when he broke through the ice on a pond. He put his horn up again and blew three different tones.

"And so now let us breakfast!" Wulf-farmer said to Thedel as he dismounted the saddle. "Tie the horses and give me the knapsack! Join us, lads . . . we have plenty." He unpacked, and the other two gawked openly, for there were sausages and thick slabs of ham and roast beef, and half a roasted goose, a large hunk of cheese, two kinds of bread, and a large metal bottle.

"Do you always live like this?!" they exclaimed. Harm laughed: "Most of the time! Don't be shy, now . . . dig in . . . it wasn't pillaged and it wasn't stolen . . . that is, not by us. The three marauders we took it from yesterday probably didn't buy it with cash money, though. Anyway, how do things look in Ödringen?"

Bolle lifted the fist in which he was holding a knife, and let it fall to the ground. "Ödringen?" he shrugged. "Ödringen no longer exists... it's in ruins . . . all rubble and trash!" As farmer Wulf and Thedel glared, he related: "For three solid weeks everything was quiet, so some folk moved back . . . Hingstmann, Eickhof, Bostelmann . . . Bruns too. The others tried to talk them out of it, but they didn't want to hear it. Then one evening, as we were just bringing in the last crop, we saw a bright glow over the town. Suddenly someone came running . . . Tidke . . . you know, Hingstmann's shepherd boy . . . and he told us that two gypsy women showed a band of marauders the way through the heathland . . . no one else was left alive."

He made an angry grimace, then suddenly laughed and spoke further: "Tidke had awoken because there was a sick foal . . . thus he was able to hide. The others were mostly killed in their sleep. All the dogs there lay dead . . . the gypsy women probably threw them poison." He took a slice out of the bread he was holding and stuck it in his mouth; then did likewise with a piece of roast after dipping it in the salt bowl.

When he finished swallowing, he continued: "We immediately rode out into the night and got help from all around. We were our eighty . . . and sober . . . those bloodsuckers numbered barely thirty . . . and drunk! None of them were spared . . . about twenty were shot or clubbed dead as soon as they came over the edge of the heath . . . they were trying to get into the murky underbrush. The others . . . ten or eleven . . . we caught alive and took them into the marshes."

He looked first at Harm, then at Thedel. He nodded his head and grinned: "And then we put them on trial. Tidke had to cite what was to be done to each of them . . . certainly he had the most to say in the matter . . . because his mother . . . she was already seventy . . . they cut her throat. They all screamed wildly and prayed and begged when their turn came . . . except for one of the gypsy women . . . the young one . . . who actually was very pretty except for her yellow skin and black hair. She was like a beast, cursing openly as we tied her up . . . snapping and biting all around, like a fox caught in a trap. But that did her no good, because Tidke said: 'She's the one who slammed the head of Brun's little son against the gatepost!' At first she was only going to get stripped naked and horse-whipped. But when we heard that, we hung her highest of all on the oak!"

Bolle laughed heartily: "How that old tree looked, I tell you . . . with those eleven gallows-birds hanging on it! When Ulfather saw it, he jested: 'Most appropriate, like being in the midst of a fat harvest year!' And profitable it was indeed . . . those folk had over two hundred ducats on them!"

After they had finished their breakfast, Harm set out with Thedel. They rode first to Ödringen. No house stood there anymore; all the farms were burnt out. "I warned them that it would come to this," said the farmer, "but it's still shocking to see . . . this once beautiful town! Come, I can't bear to look anymore. And everyone dead . . . all of them! Hingstmann and Bruns and Eickhofs and Bostelmann.... Mother Klaus too. How often did she give me an apple to bring home for Hermke! She had this one tree . . . none of ours grew such nice apples. What a shame!"

They stopped before the moors and Thedel had to sound the horn. It took about a quarter hour, then Klaus Hennecke and his man came out from behind the bushes. Both were armed and had a real monster of a dog with them. Harm called out their names and then they came closer; but first they secured their rifles and called the dog off.

Klaus was extremely happy to see Harm. "I was afraid you'd be dead. Yes, here everything's changed. Our father is dead . . . mother followed soon thereafter. This isn't any kind of life for such old people . . . the way we have it now here in the bogs . . . wolves live better. A few of the farmhands took off and headed for the city . . . no one can blame them.... who wants to lie around here in the shrubs and underbrush, eating linden tree bark and roots? There's no lack of meat, though . . . sometimes we shoot or trap a deer . . . sometimes a wild pig . . . but you can't call this living, the way things are now. The mind starts playing tricks on you . . . old man Mertens went and hung himself!"

Wulf-farmer, whose heart had been hardened by campaigning throughout the country and living in the wilds, nevertheless had to pull himself together when he arrived at Peerhobst Hill. "My God, how awful the people look," he thought, "and living worse than beasts in the field!" They had built themselves meager huts out of pine branches and sod, covered with reeds and sedge. They slept on straw and peat moss, and their eating utensils were made of alder wood. The women were all pale and wretched, and not one of the children had rosy cheeks or chubby legs. The men all had eyes as shifty as wildcats.

But all were happy when they saw the two men approach, for it was something new amid their wretched existence. The big farmers, who used to hardly notice Thedel, now couldn't talk to him enough.

But the farmhand, who now looked like a real soldier in his leather waistcoat and high-top boots, said little. "There's not much to tell. We've seen so much misery . . . it's unspeakable. In some districts, they've put guards on the graveyards . . . to prevent the starving from eating the dead. Outside the gates of Peine we saw a man broken on the wheel . . . he had stolen children and then butchered and roasted them. And as we passed by Greater Goltern, the Leaguer troops had recently marched through and burned the entire town, including the church tower . . . thirty-three people, old and young, perished."

Thedel continued: "Most of the time we fought through on our own, defending our beer and bread. Now and again, we'd throw in with the honest farmers living out in the wilderness and go against the rabble. Between the districts of Hanover and Burgdorf, we took forty-eight out of the world in one hour. But the best time was in Kalenberg, where we gathered a force three hundred strong, then came down on them like dogs on rabbits. That was tremendous, let me tell you!"

He was just about to continue when a cry rang out: "Hear ye, hear ye, hear ye!" The farmers sprang up, their eyes wide and clear. "Take heed . . . today we're going to have a rabbit hunt!" And so it was, as Drewes from Engensen spread the word that a train of Wallenstein troops, forty strong, was on the march. Anyone who could attend was to immediately head for Hingst mountain. "Are you coming with?" the others asked Harm. "Well, of course!" he said with a laugh. "A man needs his recreation! Thedel won't stay behind either, you can believe that. That boy can hit his target, I tell you!"

There were over one hundred and fifty farmers and field hands together on Hingst mountain when Wulf and his sidekick arrived. They weren't standing out there laughing and joking, like in the old days before the marauders overran the Wulfstead. They spoke quietly to one another and glanced around suspiciously. Also, they didn't look like proper farmers; more like soldiers and highwaymen. All were holding rifles in hand and lances over their shoulders. Most also had beards and barely looked respectable, save for Drewes, who carried himself like in the old days.

The Ödringers startled thoroughly when the Engenser turned around and they could see his face. He had become an old man! His complexion was yellow and his face wrinkled. "Naw," replied a farmer from Wettmar, when Wulf asked if Drewes had been ill. "Naw, he wasn't sick . . . he was widowed. You knew her . . . his Christie . . . her and her sharp tongue! Well, it cost her her life. When a pair of Danish soldiers took all the sausages and ham from her larder, she cursed them out so severely that one of them hit her over the head with his saber. That did her in. We all thought Drewes would be glad to be rid of her and seek out somebody younger and prettier . . . goes to show how wrong one can be. In three weeks the man has aged twenty years! It's a wretched thing . . . also, we've noticed that he's taken less interest in the general good . . . not like before. His best days are behind him, and he's become like washed out straw."

Wulf noticed it as Drewes began to speak. Already from the way he stood there, supported by the thick blackthorn staff, one could tell he was not the man of old. His words carried weight, yet lacked their former zeal . . . without spirit or strength. "Dear friends!" he started. "These days many of us have prayed to dear God: 'Give us today our daily bread!' The Lord has heard our prayer . . . he provides bread to us. Everyone should now do his part so that this day brings us

success! Everyone will receive orders from their group captain. One more thing I want to say . . . I notice our friend from
Ödringen, Wulf-fellow, is among us. I think you'll all be satisfied to let him take command for this campaign. I'm sure he's
of the same mind." The farmers nodded. "Lastly," closed the
Engenser, "I ask that you listen carefully now . . . follow orders
exactly, and see to it that the horses are not injured! Most of
them will have been taken from your neighbors. And now, go
with God!"

The group leaders and Drewes gathered around Wulf.
Jaspar Winkelmann from Fuhrberg began: "My opinion is
that we've got to get them between us. The best place for that
is by the high pines in front of the bogs. Thus, one group has
to wait until the foe has passed them, and another portion
stays to the front . . . to cut off their escape. The others must
comprise an auxiliary force to the right and left of the road .
. . that's got to be all young men who can move quietly and
quickly hide among the shrubbery." He made lines in the dirt
with his staff: "Look here, this is what I mean! Here's the train
. . . here are our people to the rear . . . and here to the fore….
here's where the auxiliary goes to each side. As the train
reaches the middle of the high pines, we sound the horns and
start to shoot as the auxiliary closes in on them from the
sides. Naturally, in each group there has to be a man who
understands the signals exactly, so our own people don't fall
into the soup and get caught in the crossfire!"

The general consensus was that this was the best plan. The
older men divided themselves into two portions and headed
out, followed by the younger. Wulf-farmer took the side next
to the bogs, because he was most familiar with that territory.
At first they all departed in a group, talking in muted tones;
but then they adjusted to single file and all conversation
ceased. Wulf led the way, then next to him prowled Thedel,
and behind him came Klaus Hennke. The weather was favor-

able; the sun had dried out the ground, but not so much so that every branch snapped underfoot. The wind was still and the air lent itself to carrying sound; if somewhere a woodpecker was working, or a bird rustled among the leaves in the dry arbor, one could hear it from a good distance.

Harm sat on the trunk of a fallen tree and had a leisurely smoke. Small birds peeped in the pine; a squirrel leapt from branch to branch; the sun shone upon the brambles, making them look as green as in June. Hennke sat on an old stump and looked as if he had fallen asleep. Thedel stood rock-steady in front of a tree trunk, his rifle to the ready, turning his head slowly from side to side, just like he was spotting deer.

Wulf-farmer was just making himself a new pipe when a jay prattled from the right. Thedel looked for a moment towards the farmer, but quickly then turned his head away again. The jay suddenly shrieked, and then a woodpecker answered, followed quickly by a thrush. The lad tapped quietly with his right foot and Klaus widened his eyes a bit. Harm sat there and kept smoking, but tilted his head somewhat. A horse neighed and a whip cracked, followed by a curse word. Then garbled talking could be heard.

Harm motioned with his hand to Thedel. "Get ready to signal!" he said quietly. The sidekick took horn in hand. "Not before I say!" whispered the farmer into his ear. The lad nodded.

"Hyah!" they heard a horseman yell, and again, "Hyah!" A horse snorted and a man blew his nose. Then came the first six interlopers on foot, rifles at the ready, their heads turning right and left in unison. Now and then they'd stop and talk in half-tones. Harm heard what one was saying: "Dammit all, what a slop this is . . . wish we were already out of it!" The farmer laughed between his teeth and thought: "You will be, soon enough!"

Three riders followed. "Nice horses!" thought Wulf. A second wagon passed, then another two men on foot, followed by a horseman, a tall, thin man with an extremely small head. The farmer stood and trembled over his entire being. But the man had a deep voice . . . ah, so it wasn't him! Another wagon came, then another, and always more; finally, the last. Harm was ready to give the signal to Thedel to sound the horn, but then he heard another wagon clatter. He readied himself. Behind the wagon rode a fat man who was wearing a white lace collar that hung over his shoulders. He had a red nose and a double-chin and looked morose.

"The worst is always saved for last," thought the farmer, and then shot. The roan made a leap, throwing the man off. "Now you can blow, Thedel," whispered Wulf, "but take cover!" The bugler placed himself behind an uprooted tree and let fly: "Tirrah Toot! Tirrah Toot! Tirrah Tooooot!" Then Thedel took his rifle and ran quickly to the fore, aiming a good moment before pressing the trigger. He then looked back at Harm, laughing as he hastily reloaded.

"Tirrah toot!" answered from below, and shots rang out all around. Now and then one could hear a curse and a scream, short laughs in between, shots from above and shots from below. Then a man rode up, chalk white in the face. He stayed for a moment in the same sitting position after Thedel shot, then fell to the side, and his horse dragged him through the mud. Behind him came another rider, hanging onto his reins with one hand and holding his head with the other. Harm waited until he was three paces away, held up his pistol, and shot him out of the saddle altogether.

The shots became scarcer, and the cursing and screaming stopped. "Looks like it's over!" called Wulf to his sidekick. The lad nodded. "Let's wait awhile," added the farmer. Thedel loaded the rifle and pistols as the other man filled his pipe and fired it up. "Now you can sound the all clear!" he called to him. "All-Uut? All-Uut?" bugled Thedel. After awhile the hornsmen below answered with the all-clear.

The farmer grabbed his rifle and went onto the cor-duroy.[36] Farmers came out of the pines from all directions. Everyone nodded to Harm: "That went smoothly!" He nod-ded back: "First catch hold of the loose horses . . . the other stuff isn't going to run off!" Everyone laughed. But then they pulled long faces as he ordered: "And then we have to bury the bodies and push the wagons into the undergrowth. The cash and other objects of value go to Drewes . . . he'll decide the distribution. Whoever has had a horse stolen gets first choice. Leave me a good rifle . . . I don't want any of the money."

He looked around at the men who stood near: "Everybody in one piece?" Someone called: "Yeah, except Ludolf Vieken got nicked . . . but he's a full-blooded bachelor, and can easi-ly spare a few drops!" Everyone laughed heartily.

They had gained sixty-six horses, a wagon full of sausage and ham, and eleven more wagons with oats, meal, and bread . . . not counting the cash, clothing, and weapons. A young man cried out: "Boys, who's buying the first round for this effort?" Everyone laughed and Harm answered: "Drewes and I will . . . that so, Drew-fellow?" The latter gave a weak laugh.

Wulf continued: "There's certainly more to life than work! But tonight it's too late . . . we still have much to do, and many of us have a long trip home. Tomorrow, however . . . the sin-gle men who can make it should meet at the Engenser Pub . . . and bring their girls. But come armed too! The others who have to stay home tomorrow will get their turn next time."

"So now let's get to it!" he urged. "By tomorrow, no evi-dence of what happened here can remain. The wagons have to go into the brush, and whatever else is lying around must be buried. After butchering swine, it's clean-up time!" All

36. A road constructed of logs laid down crosswise, usually in marshy or rain-soaked muddy areas.

again laughed and set to their work in a jovial manner. One hour later, as the moon arose, the corduroy was as clean as on the previous morning.

The next afternoon, all the young folks met at the pub in Engensen. They danced so that the hall thundered! Wulf-farmer made sure that no one drank too much, and that sentries stood watch at the inn, as well as in all directions around the town. He himself manned the entrance, smoking and drinking a sip of beer now and again from the stein he kept nearby.

A girl caught his eye; she was just about eighteen years old, with a complexion of milk and honey, hair like golden straw, and grown slender as a reed. She was dancing with a gawky farmer's son who had a face like a potful of mice. Each time she danced past Harm, she looked at him as if she wanted to lay her heart at his feet. It was Drewes' second daughter, Wieschen; she had a reputation as white as cotton, and more than one of the village boys had come away with a fat lip after trying to steal a kiss from her.

As a new song played, she danced the round but once; as she neared the Ödringer, she broke off from her partner, saying: "I can't go on . . . heavens, what a thirst!" Harm offered her a drink. She blushed fully, laughed and curtsied: "Thank you, kind sir!" He looked at her and tilted his head towards her dancing partner: "Is that your betrothed?" She shook her head: "No, I don't have one yet," and gave him a look like before.

But then the innkeeper shouted: "Closing Time!" and the young folks stopped in the middle of the song. Wieschen gave Harm her hand and said: "Come visit us sometime, Wulf-fellow . . . ever since mother died, father is so out-of-sorts. Well now, good night and good journey!"

Harm still felt the effects of the beer when he retired to the hayloft and lay down in the straw. As he drifted off to sleep,

the sound of the song that the young folks had sung last still
echoed in his head:

> *"Come in the dead of night,*
> *Come around one!*
> *Father's asleep, Mother's asleep,*
> *I sleep alone!"*

CHAPTER 7

~

The Warwolves

Harm stayed for awhile in the moors. From the large store of booty that he had earned during campaigning, he distributed several thalers among all the land wanderers that he encountered (that is, as long as they weren't robbers or murderers). The instructions he gave were to leave word with Drewes in Engensen, or elsewhere when necessary, as to where two men with whom he had business to conduct could be found, one of them called 'Holy Cross' and the other 'Suckling'.

He now spoke with Ul-father about the life that the Ödringers were living on Peerhobst Hill. "The worst of it is," he said, "that they just wait around for the war to end, wallowing in hunger and inactivity. That's wrong! We must act as if we plan to stay here forever and three days! But talk alone won't accomplish anything. That's why we . . . the two of us . . . are going to build a right proper house . . . also put some land under the plow, so far as it goes. You just watch how one after another will follow in our footsteps!"

The old man nodded: "You're absolutely right! I was thinking the same thing . . . even though I could die today or tomorrow. Nevertheless, it's a sin to keep one's hands in one's lap and waste the days our Lord God grants us. And this vicinity isn't all that rough! Even during wet years, the water doesn't rise too far . . . and the ground is good. Once a path towards the river is made and the shrubbery cleared, then you'll see all that will grow here!"

There was a great buzz among the hills as word spread: "Wulf-farmer and Ul-father are building themselves a solid house!" And sure enough, barely were the crossbeams up before other farmers followed suit. It was joyous to behold, how the men again walked upright, and how bright the eyes of the women grew, and how nicely the children blossomed; for all now had something to dwell upon other than their misfortune.

Wulf spared no expense. He had cash a-plenty, and thus hired carpenters and furniture builders from the neighboring towns. When the house was finished, including the horse-heads on the gables and a proverb over the large entrance door, everybody agreed: "It's truly a beautiful home, with everything suitable . . . even if it's only half as big and not as colorful as the old farmhouse."

The proverb that Harm Wulf had carved into the entrance crossbeam was:

"Help Yourself, Then Our Lord God Will Help You."

That didn't suit some at first. But when Wulf-farmer then threw a house-warming, they changed their opinion. All who lived in the moors were invited, along with numerous and sundry relatives from the heathlands. Wulf provided handsomely for food and drink, and music as well. He spread the word that everyone should dress up in their best finery, as in times of the Burgdorf Martinmas festival. Thus it looked so colorful outside the house, full of red dresses, white and blue jackets, and all faces beaming with joy.

It was one of those days when the sun competes against the rain clouds, with the sun holding most of the trump cards. A fresh wind blew so that the leaves rustled amid the young oaks, while the pines and firs groaned. The wreaths of holly and the long chain of hedgerows swayed back and forth, with white ribbons fluttering and colorful eggshells clicking and clacking upon them, so amusing that the children could barely contain themselves.

As all were present, Ul-father emerged from the large doors, followed by his son-in-law. The latter had shaved his beard and wore his blue jacket with red trim and large shiny silver buttons. The older children stood together as a choir, and when Fritz Fiedel from Meilendorf gave the cue, the song 'Almighty God, We Praise Thee' rang out brightly. The men removed their hats and sang along, as did the women; there were many tears. Then Ul-father stepped forward and spoke:

> "All who are gathered here today,
> Man, woman, child . . . worker and maid,
> Malice and vicious avarice
> From home and farm have driven us...
> Thus are we by disaster hard-pressed,
> And hide like wolves in the wilderness,
> Where the bogs and moorlands cover us,
> Lest the marauders discover us."
> "At first we all, to a man, lost heart,
> We wept and wailed and fell apart...
> Thought that we'd be better off dead
> Than to live in such poverty and dread."
> "But then we regained our Courage and Will,
> Took upon ourselves this house to build,
> And with good fortune it has come to fruition,
> Under our Lord God's strength and protection."

The gathering raptly gazed at the old man, whose eyes were so happy and yet so strange; the children gawked with open mouths. No one knew what to say to Ul-father . . . it was just like in church! But then he took a deep breath, changed his expression and continued:

"And since the house now stands well,
Lacking for nothing, as you can tell,
Let us, according to the ancient way,
In leisure and pleasure end the day...
Eating what the Lord has provided,
With proper thanks, our hearts united...
Then afterwards dance and take cheer
In a glass of wine or stein of beer...
And so, dear friends, enter ye here!"

What liveliness and laughter followed! Old mother Horstmann, whom no one had heard laugh since she had to leave the old town, chuckled continuously to herself and mumbled: "Oh my, that Ul-father . . . what a headful of jokes he has!" Even Klaus Hennke, the biggest sourpuss of all, laughed out loud, long and hard. Such a festive house-warming had never been held, even in Ödringen. It would have been exciting enough, even if there had not been one drop of mead or glass of wine to appear on the tables. All were thoroughly spirited by dinner time, and afterwards, as the dance began, no one had ever seen red skirts fly higher and wilder than at the Wulf-farmer's party.

Understandably so, for he had thought of everything. Thin beer and mead were there, two kegs of lager beer, and a tobacco like no one had ever smoked; small wonder, for Drewes and his band took it some time ago from a supply column, along with 12 barrels of Spanish wine, which was as sweet as honey, and of which all the elderly men and women received a glass or two, to strengthen the heart. "I am now all of ninety years old, but I've never had such a good time in my entire life!" said the houseman from the Bollenstead, as he nodded happily to his great-grandchildren, whose cheeks were all filled with the sweet raisin bread that had been earmarked for the single ladies that Wallenstein's officers had in tow.

Even Drewes looked different than from the time before. He stood between his two daughters . . . the large and broad Lieschen, who ran the farm with her husband . . . and the slim Wieschen, who never took her eyes from the Wulf-farmer. She wouldn't dance with anyone, saying that she didn't feel up to it. Yet she looked like a rose in the morning dew and had eyes as blue as the lovely heavens; when she laughed it was as if the marsh thrushes were ready to fight. "No, Wulf-fellow," she said when he asked why she wasn't dancing, "not today . . . I don't have the heart for it. I can't fill my eyes enough with how the Ödringers celebrate . . . despite all that they've been through. Listen to how they sing! God will bless you for this!"

The dance ended at ten, but its effect lasted much longer. Thereafter one could hear men whistling at their work, and girls singing, even when they had to do a man's job (which nowadays was not rare).

For Wulf made it clear to the people that the first priority was to secure the hills so thoroughly that three hundred men couldn't storm them, and the tasks that were ignored last autumn must now be done.

Thus the fortress trenches were dug deeper and the wall extended higher. Also, pits and walls were set with closely packed and pointed stakes so that not even a cat, let alone a man, could get through. Additionally, a barrier of thorn bushes was to be made around the wall, so high and thick that the Devil himself, along with his grandmother, couldn't breach it. Wolf-runes[37] were carved into the trees in every direction around the hills; they signified: "Beware! Before you is an abyss, and should you fall in, you are doomed!" In addition to all of this, each of the two main access roads could be blocked with barricades.

37. Wolfsangel, an ancient runic symbol that was believed to ward off wolves. Historically, it appeared in Germany in various places ranging from road markers to heraldic coats of arms for families and towns.

Wulf had seen all of these measures here and there, making mental notes during his travels. For an even greater measure of security, he set up outposts in the treetops in four directions around the sand hills of the fallow lands. During the day, the young men sat there as look-outs, sounding their horns whenever danger approached.

It was not long before all who didn't wear a clean shirt, as it were, gave the moors a wide berth. Word was spreading that things were eerie around these parts. Now and again, one saw men with dark faces lurking in the undergrowth. In other places, there were two pine trees stripped of bark, with a third tree nailed across. But scariest of all: upon those trees one saw a man, or two or three, hung by the neck . . . and no one knew who they or their judges were. No one, that is, except for the farmers in the area. When the wind made this strange gallows fruit swing to and fro, they laughed and remarked: "The marsh bells are ringing nicely today!"

Since the winter was mild, all sorts of work could be done. The farmers cleared the brush from Peerhobst Hill and divided the land equally by lottery. They made trenches and walls around the adjacent pastures, and fetched large stones out of the moors, using the iron ore in the fields to make foundations and sturdy walls.

As February came to a close for the Peerhobstlers, things looked quite different than in the autumn. Especially since nourishment was not lacking, for game meat ran in ample supply; the moors were teeming with deer, and the streams provided fish in abundance. Wulf-farmer provided for bread.

He had gathered together a secret militia of about thirty single men and organized a scouting patrol. When news came of a supply train here or camp followers with provisions there, it was not long before shots rang out and thirty-odd men with dark faces laughed throatily, saying: "Now mother has bread again, and need not slice it so thin."

Ludolf Vieken from Rammlingen, a birddog around every
quail in a red skirt, and the wildest dancer at the harvest festival (or wherever else a fiddle could be heard), was a man
who gladly joined in the fray at every opportunity. At the end
of March, during a round at the Obbershagen Inn after three
supply wagons of the Imperial forces had been captured, he
remarked: "We have a strapping new baby boy on our hands
here who still lacks a name. Our leader, he's called Wulf . . .
and a real wolf he is . . . for wherever he bites, thirty-three
holes appear! Therefore I say that we should call ourselves the
'Warwolves'! As an insignia . . . wherever we have fought evil
. . . we leave behind three axe cuts . . . one to the left, one to
the right, and the third diagonally across. No one must know
about it, save us . . . the three-times-eleven . . . as we
Warwolves shall call ourselves. Whoever betrays the brotherhood and opens his mouth about us . . . he should hang with
the willow around his neck between two mangy dogs . . . until
folk can't tell which stinks worse."

"Now that's an idea with head forward and tail behind . . .
that dog hunts!" said their leader. "What our Wolf-brother
said there . . . as if merely joking in his beer for fun . . . that is
reasonable and intelligent. Thus here we stand, three-times-
eleven men, and the Devil incarnate wouldn't scare us, even if
he now stood in our midst . . . for what could he do to us, we
single men with no children or attachments? Ludolf Vieken
aside, of course . . . the cock of the walk whenever hens are
nearby."

They all laughed like green woodpeckers; that is, except for
Vieken, who made a duck's face and was scratching himself
behind the ear. When things quieted again, Wulf continued:
"So . . . we've got to defend the married people . . . the widows
and orphans . . . and the old folks. But that means we've got
to have more . . . up to a hundred men . . . all chaps like us,
who can laugh in the face of flying lead. Therefore each of us

must seek two or three good friends . . . they are to help out when the need arises. They should all be bachelors . . . and no only son of a widow. And if anyone has a girlfriend with child, he should think long and hard before throwing in with us. If such a man comes to misfortune, then it will be our duty to make sure the woman and child do not fall into poverty. So let us now take an oath of brotherhood: 'Through Want and Good, through Death and Blood, One stands for All and All for One!' And all of us stand for those who live in the moorlands, and are of our kind!"

The innkeeper's son, one of the three-times-eleven, had to fetch the large ceremonial glass. Beers were shoved to the side, and a lordly wine (which was cheaply acquired on the road between Burdorf and Celle) appeared at the table. They all stood and linked their arms together in a tight circle. Harm took the glass, drank from it, then gave it to Ludolf Vieken, who passed it on to the next man; thus it made the rounds until empty. Then Christian Gronhagen from Hambuhr, the quietest one of them all, and a man despite his twenty years, sang the Warwolf Verse that suddenly came to him. Their leader put a white staff on the table, also his long dagger and a willow noose, and repeated: "When the staff calls,[38] the dagger falls and stings, or else the willow swings!"

They elected Vieken second-in-command, then determined where and when they would regularly meet; also, in which manner one would pass news to another, without each messenger needing to know or relay all details. Then they departed. The Wulf-farmer stayed awhile with the innkeeper's son, for he had a message from Wietze: the two men he sought had been seen in Ahlden. Amid all the work and tasks, he had forgotten about those men for awhile. However, now

---

38. A staff or baton was passed around from house to house, or town to town, whenever a meeting was called. The color of the staff, or ribbons attached to it, would signify what type of gathering it was to be and the level of emergency.

they again occupied his mind, and he promised himself to not let it go until he had paid them their just reward, down to the last penny.

The next day Thedel arrived with Gripper at noon, and the three set out. Lately he had the dog with him most of the time, for he discovered that the hound had a keen nose and could pick out the scent of one man amidst one hundred. Had it not been for the dog, he wouldn't have rooted out the gypsy and six sneak thieves from the cave in Bissendorf woods. That band of swine had been making the neighborhood unsafe, and as a warning to all dishonest folk, they wound up hanging on the birch trees in front of the town. One other time, were it not for the dog, he would have fallen into the grasp of Tilly's troops, who were chasing him after he (again) had taken the bread from their mouths and the beer from their gullets.

It was one of those early spring days in which the morning fog shaded the sun for as long as it could. Thus it was almost eleven o'clock before the sun came out for its walk. But then the weather became all the nicer, so that even Thedel (who usually concentrated fully on his work) noticed every little thing that lived on the ground, and all that wove through the air. The farmer was no less enthralled. "Boy!" he said, "this is a day that our Lord God spent some time on! If it were at all possible I'd prefer to not have to bend a finger . . . and I guess you'd also rather see if you couldn't meet up with Hille Ehlers in some shaded place where no one would bother you, eh?"

Thedel rode up to him with the sun in his face, and his ears appeared for a moment like two corn poppies. He said nothing, but sighed to himself . . . as long and deep as a horse's tail, so that Harm laughed heartily.

"Well. . ." he said, for he saw that his sidekick had an expression on his face like that of a hedgehog when the dog comes a-barking, "what is not yet can yet become. For now, we have other work at hand. 'First work, then play!' as Ludolf Vieken said when he knocked out three of Christian Kassen's teeth, and then retired to the lawn with his dance sweetheart. But when two certain people have just learned to fly . . . that is, without becoming heavenly angels . . . then Thedel Niehus, you should have your own house . . . with a lordly bed and a pretty wife in it . . . if that's your wish. And I wouldn't be surprised if she was called Hille from front and Ehlers from back . . . arms like two pine saplings . . . and hair like that grass over there, where the sun touches it just so."

He held onto his dapple (he had neglected to keep the horse black with the passing of the time) and suddenly said: "What's wrong with that dog? He's acting as if someone is out there . . . he doesn't hold his head so oddly and stand on three legs without reason. Let's go take a look!" Harm rode slowly to the spot and looked at the tracks, then said: "Sure enough! Just like I thought . . . a person! Looks like a woman . . . going barefoot . . . but no gypsy woman . . . the big toes point inward. She's young . . . tall, and thin . . . and she's had a fright. She could be sick too . . . she's stumbled twice going from the birch tree to here . . . and then she sat down. Let's go see who she is . . . can't be far . . . the tracks are fresh in the sand, and no moisture has settled in them yet. Gripper, here! Thedel, take the hound onward and give me your horse . . . but keep your hand on your pistol . . . the Devil may be at play."

He took the reins of Thedel's pale in his left hand and made ready his pistol, while Thedel followed the scent, dog collar in hand. Wulf followed on their heels, keeping a sharp lookout for any thorn in the grass, as it were. They reached an old cemetery that was overgrown with junipers and shrubbery; the dog then stood fast. Thedel grabbed under the dog's collar with his left hand, held a pistol in his right, and progressed step by step. Behind him, Wulf-farmer waited with cocked weapon ready.

"It's no hedgehog or polecat or adder," thought the farmer, for Gripper was wagging his tail. But then the hound jumped back; a woman cried out when Thedel pushed the bushes to one side. She screamed so frightfully that it went through Harm's bones, right to the marrow. As he rode closer, he saw a girl lying on her knees, hiding behind some of the stones, with her hands folded across her throat. She had an expression as if someone were holding a knife to it. She was shivering over her entire body and cried: "Oh God! Oh God! Oh God! Don't hurt me . . . don't hurt me! They killed my dear father . . . my good mother too! For the sake of our holiest Lord Jesus' suffering and death, please don't hurt me . . . just let me die here!"

Thedel pulled the dog back and made an extremely unhappy face; the farmer likewise looked around nervously, as if his own life was at stake. Then he put away his pistol, held his right hand in the air, and called from over the neck of his dapple to the girl: "We harm no one except miscreants. We are honest and just farmers and have ourselves suffered enough. Don't be afraid!" He pointed to the dog: "Look how Gripper wags his tail! Whoever he does that to need fear nothing. Look, girl . . . the hound wants to lick you. Right, my boy . . . good Gripper! That poor girl doesn't need to cry! Thedel, let him go!"

The dog went tentatively towards the girl with ears down, licked her feet, then her face, and grunted and whined. Suddenly the girl took him in her arms and hugged him tight, then cried pitifully and called out as she looked at the two men: "Oh God be praised and thanked! Yes, I can see in your eyes that you are righteous folk and won't harm me!"

Then she fell face forward and remained thus, her long hair, red as a dry juniper bush in the sun, spread out before her. Wulf dismounted and gave Thedel his horse to hold. He picked up the girl and brought her to where the sun had dried the peat moss. He took off his jacket, folded it up, and put it under her neck. Then he bent a juniper bush down, cut it off, and positioned it so that it shaded the face of the maiden. For a moment he looked closely as he kneeled beside her: she had dark circles under her eyes; her cheeks were sunken; one could see all the tendons and veins in her neck; her lips were chalk white.

He shook his head and stood up. "She's half dead from hunger and shock." He opened his saddlebag, took out a bottle, poured a little wine in his hand and knelt down beside her. After he had let a little fall on the lips of the girl, he rubbed the rest on her nose and temples. She opened her eyes, made a face like when she first saw the men, then tried to get up. But she fell again onto the jacket and said weakly: "I'm so hungry . . . oh so hungry!"

Harm already had his knapsack in hand. He sat beside her and broke off a tiny piece of bread; he noticed her mouth water when she smelled it. He gave it to her and said: "Slowly! The slower you eat, the more you can have." But she couldn't get it down no matter how much she swallowed and gagged. So he poured some more of the Spanish wine out into his hand and gave it to her. When she had it all down, she sighed deeply, then smiled dumbly and trembled with both hands towards the bread. The farmer took her in arm as if she were a small child and held the bread in such a manner so that each time she could only bite off a piece as big as a fingernail. In between he gave her just as small a piece of salted meat, and now and then some wine.

It truly lightened his heart as she ate and drank, evermore peacefully, until she didn't appear so blue under the eyes and could hold her hands steady. Then he laid the bread and meat upon the knapsack lid, put the bottle next to it, and said: "So . . . you're at the point now where you can finish on your own without eating yourself sick." He then took his arm from her shoulders. The girl looked at him in such a way that he suddenly felt as if his collar were too tight; for he now noticed how lovely she was, despite her disheveled hair and dirty face and cuts and bruises. Then he noticed, too, that she looked down at herself and discreetly tried to close her blouse under her neck; but it was ripped all over and her bodice hung on her so that he saw the three half-red and half-black scratches that went across her breast.

"Thedel!" he called. "Take the high ground on the knoll . . . we have to be on guard!" The lad followed his orders. Wulf took off his scarf and put it over the girl's shoulders from behind and back, so that she could tie it across herself. "It's still a bit chilly," he said; "you could come down with something." Likewise he removed his shoes and took off his stockings and gave them to her, with the words: "They're well-worn . . . but when a man only has a cow, he can't sell goat's milk!" He then laughed.

But when she looked at him openly, his head was like that of a laying hen and he felt as if he were sitting on an ant hill. Her hands dropped and her eyes welled up; she suddenly took his hand in hers, bent over and kissed it, so that it became wet with her tears.

He took her by the shoulders, nearly roughly, and straightened her up. "Are you full now? We have plenty . . . the cat won't drag our stomachs behind the gooseberry bushes! But let's see if we can find water somewhere . . . I don't have a mirror . . . but I do have a piece of ribbon . . . you can do up your hair a bit." He craned his neck: "Down there are some alders . . . wherever they are, a brook must be near . . . it will provide clean water for fixing yourself up. Let's go!" He took her on his arm and walked her to the spot. "How light she is!" he thought, and then he felt an odd tightening in his chest when her breath and the scent of her hair passed him. Odd too, the way his heart seemed to be affected by how quickly her heart was beating, compared to his.

Thus he was very glad to put her down by the brook. But before he left her alone, he broke off an alder branch, measured it against her foot, then said laughingly: "And now I've got to go play the cobbler! Let me know when you're finished here."

Thedel didn't know what to make of it when the farmer ordered: "Give me your boots!" His eyes grew sharp when Wulf took his knife and cut off the top brims of those boots, Thedel's pride and joy! But then when he cut those open, poked holes in them, and pulled a piece of rawhide string through, Thedel knew the meaning of it. He then said: "At first I was going to get mad . . . I thought you were laying a prank on my doorstep."

The girl nearly laughed when Wulf gave her the stringed shoes, but gladly accepted them, for she was walking in stocking feet over the heath like a cat on a wet hallway. "Everything all right?" asked the farmer, and she nodded. He took her and lifted her onto the dapple, then sat behind her. "Thedel, ride ahead!" he called. "My line of sight isn't clear."

The skies grew ever brighter; the woodlarks sang out from above; the tree pipits soared upwards, then twittered and landed again; the bog myrtles were blossoming; here and there a willow bush lit up in yellow. Harm let the dapple proceed at walking pace because, as he said: "Even though we've tarried unexpectedly, the time spent is of no great concern."

His heart was light. He thought it was because he had rescued a piteous soul. But when he caught a scent of her hair . . . and heard her heart pounding . . . and looked at her cheeks . . . so lean and pale, yet still so beautiful . . . and the small fine ears that appeared now and again from under her red locks . . . and the thin white throat emerging from the red scarf . . . and when he felt her hand, which lay on his thigh . . . and her left arm around his waist . . . well, then he didn't know whether it was nice or terrible. All things considered, it suited him quite well.

"You see those storks?" he asked her, motioning with his head in the direction of the wold, where two forest storks blinked and flashed in the sun as they circled above it. The girl nodded. "That's where we're heading. There you'll be able to get a good rest . . . afterwards, we'll take care of everything else. Just so you know . . . I'm called Harm and farmed the Wulfstead in Ödringen . . . until the day that the Devil loosed his minions upon us. And now we live like the wolf in the woods and the eagle over the moors . . . except we don't hunt innocent rabbits . . . we're not that sort . . . we hunt only the fox and all other such beasts. And that's Thedel Niehus . . . the same goes for him . . . except that for awhile now, he's left his heart behind in some maiden's apron . . . and good for him . . . he who desires a thing will have it, in good time."

He paused, puzzled as to why he was showing half of his cards to this girl who he didn't know . . . neither where she was from, nor what was up with her. But he noticed that his tongue galloped along of its own accord. "What is your name, then?" he asked. "Johanna," she replied. He then asked: "And what are your plans now?" She turned her face to him and looked him in the eye: "Let me stay by you . . . I can do all kinds of work . . . and gladly . . . whatever is needed! What else can I plan . . . if I can't stay on with you? Please . . . please, take me on. Can't your wife use a maid?"

"Listen," he said, and his voice was suddenly as if buried in ashes; "I have no wife. I'm a man like that lone eagle there in the sky. But I can see that there is no guile in you . . . if you like it by us, you can stay . . . with pleasure. So don't worry. For the time being we won't be going straight home . . . I have some business in this vicinity . . . the kind of business for which it's better that you should travel as if a man. I notice that you can handle yourself on the back of a horse. More won't be necessary."

"I will do whatever you want me to!" she answered, and he had to glance down when he saw the look in her eyes.

"And now . . . so you know who I am," she said. "My father was a preacher in Bavaria. We lived in peace until the war came. Then half the town went up in flames and most of the people were killed. My father then sought another post, so we came into this area, where the people were very good to us . . . better than elsewhere. Father wanted to go to Hannover because he thought that perhaps he could obtain a modest position there . . . he had letters from councilmen and other lords of good reputation. But then some of Tilly's solders seized us. A gypsy girl for whom I once cleaned a nasty ulcer . . . she told them what religion we were . . . and then they were like the Devil incarnate. I'll tell you all of the details some other time . . . I can't stand to think about it now. I had to witness my father being beaten to a pulp . . . when my mother cursed them, they drowned her in a fountain trough . . . before my very eyes. To this day, I don't know how I got away. I only know they were all drunk . . . and I continued to run and run . . . and only regained awareness when I fell into the brush. Then I ran again . . . as much as I could . . . and fell again . . . and lay there until I recovered my wits . . . subsisting on grass and roots . . . avoiding all contact with people. Then you found me."

She threw her arms around his neck and laid her head on his chest: "You'll retain me, you say? You are so good . . . so nice!" She cried so that her tears fell onto his legs, and he felt them through his pants. He let her cry, for he saw that it did her good.

Just as they reached Jeversen he said: "So . . . now we have to dismount. Thedel, check how the bees are flying, and whether we're upwind or down. Meanwhile we'll stay in the brush. Also, see to it that you acquire some men's clothes that will fit this maiden, and everything that goes with them. But don't tell anyone anything more than need be known by the heath!"

He lay his coat down for the girl, folded his jacket and made a pillow out of it for her head. "Lie down and sleep . . . I'm going to wash up a bit. Gripper, here! The dog will see to it that you sleep undisturbed. I'll be very near." He wrapped her in the coat and bedded her down. She smiled at him like a small child that was being tucked in, then sighed and closed her eyes. The dog sat next to the girl, sniffed her, and then also lay down; but he kept his head erect.

Harm had already smoked a second pipe when Thedel returned with the clothes and accoutrements. He whispered: "The wind has changed! In the pub, there are four strangers holding sway. The innkeeper has a face like a brown owl . . . they've beaten him so . . . and now they are drunk and molest the women. No one is doing anything because they brag that many more of their people are right behind them."

Wulf knocked out his pipe. "Hmmm," he said, "have Wibert Warnekens and Heine Hilmers been told? Good! Then let's not delay having a look at these guests." He took the clothes and went towards the brush. Gripper wagged his tail so that it rapped strongly on the ground and woke up the girl. "Here," said Wulf-farmer. "Thus far you've been a Johanna ... . but now you must make a Hans of yourself. I'll retreat and let you change. Thedel and I . . . we have business in the town. Would you rather stay with the hound and horses . . . or do you want to come with us? But let me warn you . . . there will be dead men on view. You want to come? Good! A man has to have full panoply . . . here's a knife . . . and take that pistol there . . . it's loaded. So, we're off. Gripper, don't you dare let anyone near the horses!" The dog hung his ears down and watched until Harm and company were around the corner.

"Listen up, Hans!" said Harm. "There are louts in the pub again . . . molesting people. We can't tolerate that . . . so we've got some dirty work ahead. You keep behind me . . . understand? As the bough starts to knot, you can take hold of my hand." He looked towards the junipers and waved. "Well! Did we disturb your supper?" he said to the two young men standing there who were looking at the girl. "This is a good friend. Look alive, now! Whoever wants to catch ravens can't wait until they take wing."

They went through some oak shrubs, climbed over a break in the hedge, and crossed over toward the pub. Then Wulf said: "You two go on alone and see to it that you remain by the side doors. When someone throws a pail of water out of the main entrance, that's the signal for us to enter. You have your lead billy saps, right? In a respectable pub one must work cleanly!"

The two farmers' sons laughed between their teeth and went forth. Harm, Thedel, and Johanna climbed over the fence, ducked under the windows of the inn, and then the farmer said: "So, Thedel . . . put on your dumbest peasant face."

Harm remained standing behind a stack of firewood, and the girl stood behind him. He felt her breath on his neck. A raucous laugh arose from within the pub, then a woman squealed. Harm felt it as the girl behind him shivered over her whole body. He turned to her and whispered: "Are you afraid?" "Not afraid . . . something else!" she said, and he nodded back.

At that moment, the innkeeper's wife poured a pail of water out from the large doors. "Come!" whispered Wulf. At first he whistled the Brambleberry Song, then laughed loudly as he entered the house. A man sat by the fire holding the youngest daughter, a child of twelve, in his mitts. Another was pulling a serving girl back and forth. Two others, who had a good load on by this time, stood there and drank.

"Well! Things are mighty jolly in here!" called the Ödringer loudly. "A good evening to all!" He then slugged the bloke who was sitting by the fire over the head with the short lead sap that he pulled from his left sleeve; the man fell dead against the andirons. Barely had he hit the floor when his partner, who held the servant girl in his arms, joined him with a thud (Wibert Warnekens had served him well). The two other riders looked on dumbly, and before they grasped the situation, they too lay across the floor; Wulf knocked the one and Heine Hilmers the other.

After the flett had been cleaned up, Wulf laughed and said: "So, now that that's behind us, and we're among friends, let me buy a round!" Then he asked the girl quietly: "Do we frighten you?" She looked at him with bright eyes and shook her head. "Well, let's have supper . . . then we'll be needing our sleep . . . especially you, since you haven't had a chance lately." Harm turned to the barman: "Have you a vacancy for three, my good fellow?" The innkeeper nodded and replied: "Plenty of room for you! That is to say, Thedel can sleep with our farmhands, and you two take the guestroom."

When Harm was alone with the girl he said: "So . . . now lay down, Hans. You don't need to take off much . . . we have to leave early. You can sleep peacefully . . . an entire town guards us. Wherever we are, you will be protected. There is no blood on our hands . . . at most, on our cudgels . . . and that matters little. A knave must be greeted as such . . . and the best way to rid the lawn of a wasp nest is with boiling water."

Johanna had barely put her head down and she was already asleep. At first Wulf-farmer couldn't get to sleep, and he didn't want to stir, lest he awaken the girl. All sorts of thoughts swam in his head; finally, his eyes did close. He slept until the innkeeper's wife came in and said: "It's almost five and breakfast is ready." With that she withdrew and left the small oil lamp on the stool.

Harm stood up quietly and cupped the lamp in his hand as he entered the bedroom. "Too bad," he thought, "she's sleeping so soundly!" But then the girl sighed deeply, lifted her hands in the air, and opened her eyes. When she saw the farmer standing there, she whispered "Oh . . . it's you!" and she laughed. "Soon you must get up," he said, "but stay in bed a moment longer. I'll go get you a bowl of soup and some washing water. After that, I'll acquire a horse for you . . . we want to travel quickly."

By first light they had reached a one-building farm. "We'll stay here until noon," said Harm. "Say there, Hans old chum . . . you ride like a real stable hand!" Johanna laughed: "The children of preachers learn everything . . . except how to be pious! And I can also shoot . . . along with cooking and sewing." Wulf laughed: "Well, I have to admit then, you know more than I do!" She laughed again, and he thought: "If she keeps laughing like that, then my fate is sealed!"

The farm was called Wodshorn. The farmer spoke hardly a word, and his wife not much more. But the guests lacked for nothing. Around nine o'clock a farmer's son approached and spoke to Harm in private. He then told Johanna: "Now we have to stay here until tomorrow. The best thing to do is, you go back to sleep . . . and I will too. The wise eat and sleep today for tomorrow in advance. You can speak freely with the wife . . . she knows everything. She has a heart of gold . . . but has lived through frightful things. That's why she doesn't say much and has forgotten how to laugh."

Around noon the girl awoke. The farmer's wife stood before her and said: "If you'd rather remain resting, I'll bring you your food in bed." Johanna shook her head: "No, then I would be ashamed. I'll get up." The woman smiled: "Would you rather put on girl's clothes? I have some that will fit you. Here . . . in this house . . . there are nothing but people who speak no more than they should. Tomorrow you can dress again as a stable boy."

She laid out a red skirt, a vest, socks and shoes for her, along with everything else that goes with it. When she returned awhile later to the room and saw the girl standing there, all done up, she nodded with pleasure. But then suddenly she took the girl in her arms, kissed her, and cried on her shoulder: "I had two daughters . . . healthy and beautiful girls . . . twins. Both were found dead in the woods last year. If you're not accepted in Peerhobstel then come back here. You will be treated like a daughter." She wiped her eyes. "Oh, what good is sobbing? There are many others who have suffered likewise . . . not the least of which is Wulf-fellow. I want to tell you about it . . . eventually you must know."

The girl listened and barely drew a breath as long as the woman spoke, though the tears rolled down her cheeks. "Yes," said her husband as he entered the room, "Wulf-farmer . . . you should have seen him in earlier years . . . everyday was a holiday to him . . . but now, he's like a gray wolf that scavenges the moors . . . only satisfied when there is blood to taste."

After lunch, during which hardly a word was spoken, Johanna helped the wife around the house. Then they both sat on a bench in the backyard and knitted. The sun shined warmly; narcissus bloomed in the grass; yellow butterflies wafted along; a magpie sought twigs for her nest; song thrushes argued in the woods; two short-toed eagles flew over the wold, shrieking loudly.

Wulf-farmer was gone with Thedel for two days. He returned looking tired, with dark eyes and narrow lips. "It was a wasted trip . . . nothing came of it," he said. "Today, I'm too tired and just want to sleep. We'll leave for Peerhobstel early in the morning."

During the night storms passed through. Johanna was awakened by them and startled, but since she was next to the wife and heard Gripper breathing strongly and steadily by the door, she soon fell back asleep. When she put on the man clothes in the morning, the wife packed the girl clothes together and made a bundle, saying: "So! These are for you, my daughter! And don't forget that Wodshorn always has a room and a place at the table for you!"

It turned out to be a beautiful morning: the black grouse were on the move everywhere; the cranes boasted; the lapwings called; the jacksnipes complained. The bog myrtles which covered the glen were vividly red; here and there grew a willow shrub that looked like an open flame. A herd of deer moved over the heathland, stood still as the three riders came into view, and then bounded quickly towards the moors.

As they rode over the high heath near Fuhrberg, they heard the cry of a wolf behind them. The farmer turned and said: "That's our people!" When he replied back with a wolf-call, two riders approached immediately from out of the brush. They were Ludolf Vieken and Christian Groenhagen. "Well, you're up early, Ludolf!" Wulf greeted him; "or didn't you even get to bed yet?" That wild hound grinned: "Oh, I got to bed . . . but not my own, mind you! Anyway, it's a shame you weren't with us yesterday. We had a fine expedition. But we'll pass by it shortly, and you can see for yourself." Vieken glanced over at Johanna. Harm caught the look: "This is a friend of mine, named Hans," said the Ödringer. "Hmmm…" mumbled the Ramlinger; he was about to smirk, but broke it off when he saw that the Wulf-farmer wasn't inviting such mirth.

He rode to the fore with the farmer and whispered something to him. Harm then let him ride onward and asked Johanna: "Hans, do you have the stomach for it when the birch trees have rotten apples hanging? The world now has several fewer marauders. I have to go there . . . if you wish, you can wait here with Thedel." The girl shook her head: "I would be happy to see all birches bearing so richly . . . then folk of pure heart would fare better." The farmer nodded.

At the point where the footpath cut across the main road, quite a few high birches stood next to one another. Five men and two women were hanging from them. There was an upright Wolf-rune carved into the bark above each of them. The eldest man, a bloke with a black beard, had a placard tied to his hands with the following words written in red chalk:

> "*Three-times-eleven make thirty-three,*
> *The Warwolves, thus are we!*
> *By this sign, let our message be sent*
> *To those of greed and ill intent!*"

CHAPTER 8

~

The Reapers

Wulf and his companions remained on the Viekenstead in Fuhrberg until twilight and didn't arrive at Peerhobstel until dark. Everyone was all eyes and ears when word spread that the Wulf-farmer had brought back a serving girl. But since she kept to herself, and everyone had their hands full with tasks of their own, no one concerned themselves about her further.

As time went on, Johanna became acquainted with the women. At first they were secretly amused by how she had red hair, spoke High German, and had hands like a noblewoman. But she worked as hard as any servant, and proved her mettle to the community when Witten-mother went to childbed; the new maid from the Wulfstead stood ably by her through the most difficult hours, and afterwards saw to it each day that the newborn twins came to rights.

The children of the town at first stood dumbly before her when she tousled their hair in a friendly manner. But they got used to her as well, and soon she had the whole lot of them around her each Sunday, telling them all kinds of stories, and teaching the young girls how to knit, sew, and darn.

"That's what we were lacking here," said Ul-father, who had taken the girl completely to his heart. "Now we have a schoolteacher . . . and none better to be had, though she be a woman. It started with storytelling, and now she's teaching

97

them reading and writing! You know what? Mother Kracken's daughter, Mieken . . . that's a serving girl for us. Then Johanna will have more time for the children . . . not to mention the sick, who she understands like a learned doctor." Wulf-farmer was very satisfied with that.

One day Gripper stepped on a blackthorn and his paw became infected; as Harm held onto the dog, Johanna cut open its paw, then cleaned and bandaged the wound so well that the farmer remarked: "Tell me, is there anything you can't do? You can ride . . . you can shoot . . . you're equal to the task of housework . . . you understand livestock . . . can handle yourself around sick people . . . and on top of that schoolmistress, midwife, and gardener. It's a joy to behold! Where did you learn it all, girl?"

She blushed and said: "I had to learn to ride as a child, because I accompanied my father when he visited the sick. And I was taught shooting by the old local magistrate, God bless him! He said: 'A woman needs to be able to protect herself even more than a man, for she has more to lose than just her life.' The other knowledge probably stems from my father intending to be a doctor at first . . . later he decided to follow a different calling. Also, the teacher we had back then, well . . . he was better at patching pants than teaching children . . . so my father took over that task and I had to accompany him there as well. My mother taught me the other things . . . especially how to handle livestock and flowers, which she understood excellently."

And that must have been true. Otherwise, it wouldn't have looked so nice around the new farm. Thedel made a beautiful fence around the gardens; and since it fit so perfectly in the spot, he put a gate between two expansive legume shrubs (which Johanna had neatly trimmed so that they appeared identical: broad at the bottom and pointed at the top) and also placed two pointed juniper bushes before the small door.

The lad carted all the needed flowers and bushes from the overgrown gardens in old Ödringen. Whenever he traveled overland with Wulf-farmer, he kept an eye out for beautiful flowers, either potted or in gardens, and collected the offshoots and sprigs. Eventually, nearly everyone came to call him 'Flower-Thedel'.

It was indeed magnificent how everything flourished in the garden. Though it was too late in the year for snowdrops, narcissi, lilies, crown imperials, tulips or peonies, nevertheless the cowslips bloomed nicely, and by June all corners of the hedgerows were filled with wild roses. Ivy climbed over the entire house; the elderberry bushes by the baking house were white through and through; the wallflower shrubs shone like copper pots in the sun.

Whenever Johanna busied herself trimming the shrubbery, and the sun shimmered on her red hair... and on her bare arms which flowed out from the white sleeves . . . and her red skirt swayed as she bent over to pull a weed . . . then old man Ul would say: "That's one fine specimen of womanhood!" With that he'd nudge Harm in the ribs and wink: "If I were half my age, I'd know what to do! Or are you waiting for someone else to snatch her away from under your nose? I've seen for awhile now that she's caught your eye, and mark my words, you won't find a better wife again so easily!"

The farmer was of the same opinion; more than once he tried to give himself a shove in that direction. But then it always seemed to him as if there were a gulf between them. For what was he? Not that he felt inferior because she was more learned. But he just seemed to lose his courage when approaching her, no matter how much time they spent together. Earlier he had devoted himself, body and soul, when it came to ridding the heathland of vermin. But now when he lurked in the moors or lay in the underbrush, he thought of only one face, framed by hair as red as the evening sun upon

the pines, and of two round arms emerging from white
sleeves. He had watched with joy as Johanna regained her
color and weight; her bodice was now well-rounded, and her
skirt didn't hang so loose on the hips anymore.

One midsummer's day, Ul-father went with Thedel to
Obbershagen to visit a cousin who owned a farm there. Harm
and Johanna were alone; Mieken had returned home for a few
days because Mother Kracken was ill. It had been sweltering
hot the entire day, and it was no cooler towards the evening,
so the farmer and Johanna sat on a bench out in the garden
at twilight. He said: "We'll surely get some rain soon," as he
noticed the thick storm clouds hanging over the Halloberg
Hills. As the lightning began and increased, Wulf noticed that
the girl would startle and put her hand to her breast each time
a flash ripped through the clouds.

"Are you afraid?" he asked. She shook her head: "No, it just
makes my limbs tingle . . . I'm a little out of sorts." She did
look paler than usual, and had a look in her eye like that time
when Gripper first discovered her. Harm remembered how he
held her then in his arms and fed her like a child . . . and how
afterwards she sat in front of him on his horse and the scent
of her hair made him feel so peculiar. He looked at the hands
that she held in her lap: they had become tanned, and the
arms likewise; but they nevertheless remained delicate and
refined, though she never shirked from any task. "She is and
remains a fine young woman," he thought, and sighed so
deeply that she laughed at him.

"Now that sounded serious!" she remarked. "Is something
laying heavy on your heart?" She gave him a merry sideways
glance, and he thought: "Now or never!" But it remained a
thought, for he felt unsure of himself: "Should I just simply
reach over and embrace her . . . or would it be more proper to
first tell her how I feel?"

Then a child who had a splinter approached; thus an
opportunity was again lost. He ate little that evening . . . did-

n't know where to put his eyes . . . felt for the most part uncomfortable in his own skin . . . and was glad when it was time to go to bed. The storm had receded.

He couldn't get to sleep for quite awhile. He was aggravated with his lack of courage, but knew of no way to extricate himself from this mess. Additionally, he was worried that it would ruin things between him and the girl. Thus ran the thoughts through his mind, round and round. Finally he must have fallen asleep, for he suddenly awoke to a blue flash and tremendous thunder. The storm had returned.

The horses kicked against their stalls and the cows struggled against their bindings. He stood up, put on his coat, and went into the hallway. There he ran into Johanna, who likewise had put on her coat and emerged from her bedroom. Another flash of lightning showed her to be chalk white: "Are you sick?" he asked. She shook her head: "It's only the storm . . . it was too stuffy in the bedroom." But as the next bolt of lightning struck, followed by a violent thunderclap, she cried out, grabbed her chest, and fell towards the wall. He jumped to her quickly and put his arm around her, then led her into the living room. He sat her down on the bench near the hearth and moved in close next to her.

Lightning and thunder came as one. The girl tried to pull herself together, but couldn't suppress her scream. With that, he took her in his arms and lay her head on his chest, covering her face with his coat lapel. He remained holding her like that; now and then, when it again flashed and cracked, he patted her shoulders and spoke to her in a gentle tone, like when a young horse shies away from the juniper hedges. She lay completely still and stopped shivering. Even though the weather continued, he only felt her pulse race.

After about half an hour the lightning and thunder ceased. It rained as if poured from buckets, and the living room grew cool. He removed his coat from her face and noticed that she embraced him tightly. He no longer felt a wall or gulf between them and was sure that they belonged together, in joy and sorrow. He then did what his heart and mind told him to.

"That was a rough night!" called Ul-father, as he returned the following afternoon and entered the large living room. He had come the last stretch by foot because Thedel wanted to fetch some fir branches for spreading. Since the old man had a quiet stride, Johanna wasn't able to extricate herself from Harm's lap as quickly as she would have liked. Thus she stood there, eyes on the floor and cheeks as red as peonies, hands straightening out her apron. She finally burst out: "Only at first!" Then she put her hands to her face and laughed, and Harm laughed too . . . and then Ul loudest of all, as he realized what had transpired during his absence.

He looked from one to the other and finally said: "Well, then . . . let me be the first to wish the both of you great fortune, my children . . . for you two have been a great fortune to me!" But then he pounded his fist on the table: "This is surely a dry engagement! A man isn't even offered a glass of wine or piece of cake? Heh . . . that's not the usual custom in these parts!"

The young woman moved as quickly as she could; on the table there soon appeared a stoneware bottle with wine, clean napkins, a colorful plate with cake, a more colorful vase with an even more colorful bouquet of flowers, and three fancy glasses of the finest kind, from which the Spanish Imperial officers had intended to drink. The wine those three then drank was likewise earmarked for other people, but thereby tasted none the worse (even though Johanna said the room was spinning after drinking but half a glass).

"Harm," said the old man, as Johanna was tidying up, "one thing I'll tell you . . . the first pastor that I run into, he must come here and make things right and proper. These are wild times, and the Devil likes to play his games. Should misfortune fall . . . and your woman is then alone . . . she could wind up an itinerant beggar, for there will be some folks who begrudge her the legal right to this farm and make all sorts of trouble. These aren't times for a full-blown wedding, understand . . . the skies grow ever darker. Tilly . . . that Papist dog . . . chases the Danish soldiers back and forth. Also, pestilence is again running rampant. Let yourselves be consecrated and done with it! The main thing is this . . . that you both have peace of mind, and no longer need dread the night."

And so it was done. It was good that the farmer hurried to wed, for whenever he had to go out into the moors and play the wolf, he could at least think back on Peerhobstel without worry.

For indeed, playing the wolf was now not an uncommon occurrence. Tilly and the Danes fought over the established towns like dogs over bones, and tales of deprivation, death, and mistreatment where heard everywhere. Wherever the soldiers harvested with their battle-scythes, they were followed by marauders with their hunger-rakes. One heard gruesome tales daily of women tortured to death and butchered; whether an old crone or a baby at the breast, whatever fell into the hands of these sub-humans was turned over to the Grim Reaper.

The Warwolves therefore had their hands full. In addition to their one-hundred and eleven man night auxiliary force, a two-hundred man scouting network was added during the day. Thus the work went quickly and efficiently, and many trees along the road bore fruit that even the greediest boy would prefer to leave hang. The Warwolves marked their targets well, and treated each according to the position he deserved: soldiers with an armband received a bullet and full burial; the other rabble however were honored with the willow noose, as crow and wolf awaited their share.

One gray day in March, Wulf-farmer had business with the town authorities. Some busy-body let it be known that the

Ödringers were now Peerhobstlers, and they were not so poor, nor starving enough yet, that taxes couldn't be levied from them. That didn't sit well with the townspeople, thus Harm (as community representative) went to plead their case and try to remove this yoke from their necks.

He told the gentlemen at the administration building: "As long as we're not being protected, we will likewise not be taxed!" They called Wulf an impudent fellow, but he held his head high and continued: "We shall see if our lord Duke Christian has an opinion on the matter! Otherwise, we'd rather just burn our homes down and live by begging and stealing . . . leastwise, until someone gives us authority to skin the honest folk who are forced to hide in the moors and wasteland!"

As he went out the door, he found Thedel standing there, totally white around the nose and with eyes like a wildcat in the dark. The latter said: "Suckling and the Holy Cross are sitting in the pub, half-drunk, and Ludolf Vieken is getting them even drunker." The farmers eyes grew wide: "Really and truly?!" The lad nodded: "I myself stood behind the red-bearded dog, my hand already on my dagger. Luckily I stopped to consider that this wouldn't be your wish. They won't get away from us today, Farmer . . . like that time in Ahlden. I was already in Heessel and Schillerslage . . . from there onward came all sorts of news from honest folk . . . this time the reports were reliable, indeed!"

As Wulf accompanied Thedel to the inn, it struck him that this wasn't as big a cause for joy as it actually should have been. He thought more about Peerhobstel and his wife than about these gallows clappers. Nevertheless his pace was at first hurried. But then he caught himself, and started walking casually down the street, as if he had as much time as a stable lad who had the task of cleaning stalls before him.

He paused and asked the innkeeper's wife (who stood outside the door) about her children. But suddenly he couldn't listen to her any longer, for he now heard a voice . . . a man's voice, but high as a young stallion's whinny . . . a voice whose tone he had never heard, and yet recognized . . . for he had often imagined it during the long hours he lurked in the underbrush or rode over the heath. He thought about that afternoon on the Hingst Mountain, how he rode through the peat with Klaus Hennecken and got first wind of something burning, and all the other things. His Rose stood before him, Hermke on her skirt, and in her arms little Maria. He suddenly gnashed his teeth with a vengeance, making a noise that thoroughly startled the innkeeper's wife.

He went into the pub without looking around at the other patrons, then stood at the bar and ordered a beer. Harm listened to the small talk of the bartender with one ear, then put his mug down on the table near the door. He got his bread and bacon out of his knapsack and pulled out his knife, eating leisurely and deliberately the whole time. Then Ludolf Vieken looked up and put his right hand on the table . . . first the thumb, then the index finger, and then the middle finger sprang from his fist. Wulf-farmer was about to return the signal, but the Holy Cross shouted: "Let's have another, you old booze-hound! Then I'll buy another round, for I'd just as soon laugh as live!"

The Peerhobstler now took a close look at the men, and he imagined for a moment as if they were already stretched at the neck, their tongues hanging out of their mouths. They would not escape, for near them sat another Wulf, known as Schütte, from Wennebostel; he was Harm's half-brother, who married into a farming clan there. Also sitting there were Dettmer Münstermann and Christian Grönhagen. Hinrich Duwen and Diedrich Flebben stood by the ovens. Kurt Aschen sat on a bench, playing with a cat underneath it that kept hacking at his fingers. And there sat the two fiends, barely able to keep their eyes open, yet highly pleased when their dirty jokes and horror stories brought the company to laughter.

"Were you ever in Schillerslage, Suckling?" asked Ludolf Vieken. "There's high amusement to be had there! The innkeeper has a daughter who drives even the old men wild, I tell you! But the girl's like a nettle thorn . . . I'd like to see the fellow who plucks her maidenhead. None of us here have been able to win her favor."

Harm laughed through his teeth: first of all, the innkeeper had no daughter, only an old serving wench; second, she was a trollop; and third, she looked no better than a dead cat which has been lying out in the rain for eight days. But the Suckling pounded his rickety chest: "If anyone can, then that would be me . . . for I have outrageously good luck with the ladies!" His blackguard chum vouched for him: "Yes, that he has . . . sure enough! Like a bow on a fiddle, that is..." he continued, looking half impudent and half anxious, "when there's no other way, he doesn't fool around and just chokes them!"

The Suckling, who had just let a large mug of honey beer slide down his long gullet, laughed like a cuckoo: "Damned right, that's what I do! Why else are they here? And anyhow, an adventurous man with courage doesn't dally around for eight days, peeping like some sparrow. A little persuasion, shall we say, can be a big help!" he bragged, working his hands open and closed, like a swooping hawk its claws.

Thedel stood under the doorway, watching Harm's back. When Wulf-farmer caught the look his sidekick threw at the scoundrels, he got chills down his spine; it was as if a corpse were prattling there, rather than a living man.

Then the bloke started singing, and laughing to boot, as he squeaked:

"Oh Gallows, you house on high,
So dreadful to my eye,
So dreadful to my eye!
I cannot look, for I discern

That I shall have my turn,

Yes, I shall have my turn!"

The farmer went outside when Ludolf Vieken clicked his tongue. "The oats are nearly ready for cutting," said the Rammlinger; "their heads already hang heavily."[39] He looked towards the heavens: "It's clearing up . . . another round of mead and they'll be running after us like the hens after the rooster." He knocked out his pipe: "Early morning . . . around seven . . . we'll be over the heath past the next two towns." He filled his pipe and took a light from Harm. "A hard piece of work, this . . . bringing such drunkards to justice . . . that I can tell you!"

Wulf-farmer paid his tab. In order to kill some time, he went over to the Jew across the road and haggled over a brooch. Diedrich Flebben, Wennebosteler Wulf and Hinrich Duwen rode forth, followed by Ludolf Vieken and Kurt Aschen. The two men were between the group, and didn't seem to notice that Death incarnate sat behind each of them; they joked and bellowed the Bogeyman Song[40] which was currently making the rounds throughout the German realm.

The Peerhobstler could still hear the squeaking voice, even though the party had already turned the corner: "With hand and foot, the Emperor beats the drum!" to which some children shouted back in reply: "Ta-rum-ti-dum, you rummy-dumb!"

Harm then broke off the bargaining and paid the merchant's price, for which the latter bowed several times in thanks, as Thedel approached with his dappled.

39. A reference to *Haber/Hafer* (oats) cutting is a euphemism for vigilante justice, among southern German peasants as well.

40. A reference perhaps to a variation of the *Kriegslied gegen Karl V* (War Song Against Charles V). Charles V (1500–58) Holy Roman Emperor from 1519–56, crowned King of Germany in 1520. He was a staunch Catholic who rejected Martin Luther's doctrines in the Edict of Worms, thereby declaring war on Protestantism. These "bogeymen" songs emphasized drums and rhythm to generate mirth and martial spirit.

The farmer mounted his saddle stiffly, as if it were the first time he felt a horse's back between his legs. But after paying the toll at the city gate, he set to a gallop and quickly caught up to the other riders.

At the pub in the town of Schillerlager he remained very quiet; yet as he lay on his straw pile, he didn't get much sleep, because all his thoughts were back at Peerhobstel with his wife.

Thus it went for Harm until it was already five o'clock. Thedel sat before the door of the stall in which the two cutthroats slept. He laughed grimly: "The other has been up and about for awhile . . . he sobered up too . . . were it not for the old barn rag in his mouth, he would be making a fine racket. In the meantime I've tied his hands behind his sleeves . . . and he can't get up off the floor because I've tied a cord around his waist and into the ring on the cellar door." He spat out his chaw of tobacco. "The other one slugged down so much mead yesterday that he still doesn't know where he is . . . he probably won't be sober enough for us to deal with him until this evening."

The Wulf-farmer was served soup and bread, smoked two pipes and sent Thedel forth by six o'clock. By six-thirty, quite a few farmers came riding up. They tapped with their riding crops until the innkeeper emerged (acting as if they didn't notice the Peerhobstler), drank their warm beer in the saddle, then rode on further.

A wagon approached, creaking under its load. The driver banged three times quickly, one after another, then four times at longer intervals, and whistled: "Pull, horse, pull . . . though with mud the road is full!" Ludolf Vieken called from the inn: "Jochen! Can I get a ride with you? The beer here has shrunken my feet!" Harm then likewise stood up: "Same for me! Give me a lift! A handful of tobacco is in it for you!" He sat upon the wagon bench and looked back at the straw pile; now and then it fluttered, and from under the hay came a sound, as if a hog lay beneath.

Fog still languished over the heath. "It's going to be a nice day," said Harm's sidekick, "the Wettmar Musicians are trumpeting!" (one could hear the cranes boasting loudly from within the moors). A thresher woman saw the wagon approach, curtsied and said: "Well, then, Jochen . . . see to it that you get a good deal for your hogs!" A raven called from out of the fog, and the straw pile in the back of the wagon kept moving back and forth . "Did you hear our black brother?" said the Rammlinger to Thedel. "The ravens know they'll soon have a fine breakfast!" A grunt came from the straw. A rider trotted past, then another, and then a third. "Off to the hog market?" they called to the farmhand. He nodded and smirked.

All hundred and eleven Warwolves and almost an equal amount of scouts stood around the heathland hills. As the wagon arrived, a murmur arose and circulated. The fog parted and danced off; then two pine trees with the tops cut off became visible. There was a crossbeam attached that bound them together; a dead dog already hung on the left side, and a croaked pig to the right. Between the carcasses were two ropes that reached to the ground. There was a circle of stones around both trees, opened at the front; an upright Wolf-rune was carved into each trunk, large enough to be seen from a good distance.

The farmhand nodded to the men. He cried "Whoa!" and secured the reins, then came down off the wagon, spat, and went slowly to the rear. He then pushed the bench forward and waved to two men as he reached for the sack that was under the straw, and still moving. The men helped lay it on the ground, and likewise with another one that was there. The Wulf-farmer and Ludolf Vieken dismounted and went over to where Meine Drewes stood. The latter had two debarked willow limbs in his hand. He waved, and then it grew quiet.

All two hundred men glared at the spot where the farm-hand opened the sacks. Two men were pulled out and their foot-bands were loosened. They were then stood upon their own feet and brought before the chief judge, after which the rags were removed from their mouths.

No one made a sound, not even Thedel Niehus, who stood to the fore with Wulf-farmer, making a face like a monster. Four hundred eyes looked coldly at the two arch-scoundrels who stood in deathly fear and unable to speak, hung over and shaking like leaves.

The chief judge looked them in the face and began: "As leader of the Warwolves, I summoned you all to a legal and public meeting, on the open heath of common lands, for the purpose of holding trial over these two men. Who has an accusation against them?"

Wulf-farmer stepped forward: "I charge them with the burning death of my wife Rose, born Ul, from Ödringen . . . and our children, the minors Hermke and Maria Wulf. Also, I charge them with arson, robbery, and theft of possessions from both the living and the dead."

He stepped back and Thedel took his place, crying out: "I charge them with the burning death of my sister, Alheid Niehus of Ödringen . . . an orphan child not yet fifteen years old."

He withdrew and made space for Ludolf Vieken, who shouted: "I charge them in the name of respectable maidens and widows . . . women pregnant and in their childbeds . . . innocent girls and minor children . . . the sick and the weak . . . and all who have fallen into their hands. I shout 'Revenge!' upon them, and again 'Revenge!', and a third time 'Revenge!' I swear with seven oaths that they have earned death seventy-times-seven . . . alone by what they related through their own stupid drunken mouths in the Burgdorf Inn yesterday."

The judge looked around: "Is there anyone else with additional charges against these men, or who would speak in their defense? All are free to speak here, without fear that it will be held against them!"

It became very quiet among the gathering. The sun emerged and shined upon the faces of the two hundred men, which looked as if they were carved in stone. A raven flew by and squawked, and in the ruffled pines the titmice called cheerfully.

The three-times-eleven founding members separated from the group and murmured among themselves; then one of them went to the chief representative and said something to him.

"We hereby find," spoke the judge, "that these two shall have the willow noose placed around their necks and be hanged seven shoes high . . . as common criminals . . . between the rotting carcasses of a dead dog and a butchered sow until dead. None shall dare approach to cut them down and bury them, unless they wish to take their place!"

He broke one of the limbs and threw it behind him, then the other. The willow nooses were passed forward, at which point the Suckling fell upon his knees and cried: "Mercy!" But he got no further, for the noose was already cutting into his Adam's apple. The Holy Cross had barely whimpered: "One moment . . . I feel like I'm going to be sick!" when there he stood already, willow collar around his neck and under the gallows between the three-times-eleven men. Before the ravens crowed three times, the miscreants swung to and fro in the wind. Each had a board tied to their hands which read:

> *"We are One Hundred Eleven,*
> *Warwolves by name,*
> *These are two dogs and two pigs,*
> *To us, all the same."*

The stone circle was closed off and the men departed. The Wulf-farmer had his chin on his chest. Thedel looked back one last time and Ludolf Vieken pointed to the gallows and

said: "Look, Thedel! Your wedding bells chime!" But Thedel
said nothing and followed behind Wulf.

As they both rode through the pines, the farmer said: "So
. . . and now let's not think further about it, Thedel. When do
you want to marry? Probably today, eh? Well . . . as far as I'm
concerned, it's a go . . . put it all in order! Or have you done it
already?" He looked behind him and laughed, for the lad had
the sun at his back, and thereby his ears looked as red as on
that morning in the Jeverser Heath, when Gripper found the
girl.

"And now . . . gallop, my dappled!" called Harm to his
horse. They dashed along so that the sod flew up and the
golden plovers complained behind them. The farmer thought
about his Johanna, and the farmhand on his Hille; within the
hour both horses stood behind their feed troughs.

The next day the farmer had bright eyes again, and his
sidekick even brighter. They went into the wilderness to dig
out young fruit trees and anything else useful for the garden.
As Wulf napped behind a bush around noon, Thedel rum-
maged through some piles of rubble. He found all sorts of
tools that were still usable, likewise axes and other equipment;
then, as he pushed aside a blackened crossbeam upon which
a quantity of moss had already grown, his rake struck iron.
He found the hearth kettle-hook of the old Wulfstead, a fine
specimen not to be found far and wide. A Wolf-rune, the
house brand of the Wulf clan, was stamped upon it on the
top; on the bottom a date could be read: "1111 A.D."

"That's more valuable to me than if you had found a hundred thalers in gold, Thedel!" said the farmer. "For that, I'll
build you a house . . . and everything that goes with it! Let me
tell you something, boy . . . you've served me well and long
enough. If you and your wife want to work for me in the
meantime for the usual wages, I'd be very satisfied. But I've
been thinking about it for awhile . . . just like I didn't want to
be the vassal of the nobility, you shouldn't be my house man.

You've been much more than a loyal servant during these rough years . . . it's nothing more than right that you now become your own man . . . assuming, of course, that you can defend your pants from Hille!"

Thedel grumbled something to himself, as if the farmer were throwing him off the farm. But when he finished unhitching the horses, he couldn't run to his girl fast enough; he was whistling like a fool when he returned. Then he sat down and polished the antique kettle hook with water and ashes and found no peace until it hung in its proper place.

From then on the farmhand really attacked his work, like a fox on a rabbit. The farmer didn't know where or when his man found the time to eat and sleep; Thedel nevertheless grew rounder of face, and his beard grew appreciably with each passing week. His Hille was likewise blossoming, so that the farmer mentioned: "Girl, you keep growing like that and you'll need double the material for your skirt! You'll be an expensive wife for your Thedel." But Hille laughed and dug into the earth as if it were warm butter.

As she and Thedel prospered, thus it went for most of the other people on Peerhobst Hill. Even the children helped to clear land and turn over the earth; what earlier would have been considered shameful, namely, that a woman was hitched to a plow, was now considered recreation. There was no class separation in Peerhobstel, no farmer and farmhand, no wife and serving girl; it was a joined community of industrious folk in which everyone worked the land, for himself and for all. In all the towns around the moors the expression arose: "United, like the Peerhobstlers!" The moors were big enough, woods and pastures grew everywhere; if someone lacked seed corn, or another needed tools, he was assisted before even having to ask.

The new earth plowed better than one would have thought, particularly the sand, since a marl-bank was not too distant. The braised earth amid the alder reeds was thick like wedding soup, and where the moors were scorched and mixed with sand, it was worth the effort. Though there was no lack of weeds and undergrowth, nevertheless everything stood better than one might have hoped. When the majority of work was done, the Wulf-farmer said to the thirty-three: "And now let's build our brother Thedel his little shack! I believe it's about time."

Because many hands assisted, the house was soon finished. Thedel didn't know what to say as bed-clothes, tools, and everything else necessary when one has a house and wife, appeared of their own accord. The hundred and eleven enjoyed themselves in this task, helping him when they could, with no fear that afterwards anyone would come asking for their share back.

However, hardly any of the sworn Warwolves were at the wedding. The colored staff again passed from town to town on the prior evening, and indeed, with a red ribbon around it. Thus, the entire one-hundred and eleven had to take their positions, along with all the day and night scouts. Two large bands of marauders were confirmed as sighted in the area. One of the groups vanished into the brush near Meitz; the ravens and foxes alone knew where the rabble lay buried beneath the pines. The others, though, were overrun by Thönse, and no trace of them remained, save for the ring-leader; he found a birch where the footpaths forked, and hung there until the scavengers got bored with him.

Three days later, Ludolf Vieken pulled a great prank. He and two of the other thirty-three gave a guard of honor to some Pappenheimer[41] troopers who had come to town and bought horses (that is, at war prices). In the Burgwedeler

41. Gottfried Heinrich (1594-1632), Count of Pappenheim. (Pappenheim is a small town in Bavaria.) The Count was also an Imperial Field Marshall, renowned for his personal valor in many battles during the entire span of the Thirty Years War. His Pappenheimers were an elite force of cavalry men. Like his equally stalwart opponent Gustavus Adolphus, he was mortally wounded in the Battle of Lützen.

Woods, the riders stopped to give the horses a drink, as well as themselves - though not water, and they drank so much that the heath looked to them like a giant feather bed. Ludolf Vieken crept up from behind, saw to it that the guard didn't consider drawing another breath, then quickly cut through all the horse bindings. In the meantime, his sidekick Konrad rode to the town and fetched a mare in heat, along with a dozen men who had nothing better to do at the moment. Then Vieken rode the mare upwind from the camp, and all the horses trotted after him; the young men of Burgwedel saw to it that the troopers didn't get blisters from walking. In this manner, many farmers regained their horses in stall and didn't need to plow with their only cow.

For poverty was widespread. Danes and Imperial troops moved through the heathland, and wherever they went, afterwards the soup was thin indeed. The folk on Peerhobst Hill had it best, for the soldiers never found their way to that remote town, and miscellaneous other unwashed rabble gave the moors a wide berth.

Thus the moorland farmers were able to gather their oats in peace, without needing to constantly look over their shoulders. The harvest wreath was not lacking, and the harvest bonfire appeared as well. It arose brightly from the offerings of sacrificial sheaves that were thrown into it, according to the ancient custom. Then the farmhands and maids withdrew. Hinrich Mertens swung a long pine pole around that was brightly trimmed: it had a rooster head on top, and around it were the eared stalks of the last ground covering, along with bright ribbons that flowed in the wind. How jolly it was, hearing the children sing:

> "Wodin, Wodin, God of olden,
> Here we feed your mighty steed!
> This year only thistle and thorn,
> Maybe next year better corn!"

CHAPTER 9

~

The Church Folk

The following year saw better corn indeed, but also plenty of thistles and thorns, for the war continued and just wouldn't end. Tilly and the Danes were still tearing hither and yon, and wherever they squabbled, everything was crushed underfoot.

Duke Christian, who didn't know which side to throw in with, stood by and witnessed the devastation of the land and the plundering of the people. But he couldn't just relinquish all revenues either, and so the parliament again issued a three-fold tax levy.

When the Peerhobstler representative got the notice, he saddled his dappled and rode with Thedel to Celle. Along the way his mood grew dour; everywhere one looked, Hunger sat by the hearth fire and Pestilence was peeking in the window. Wretched huts and shacks were erected outside the walls of Celle, and refugee peasants from the plundered towns eked out their existence there through begging and stealing, even robbery and murder.

As the two Peerhobstlers and their companions (they met six more of the thirty-three along the way, so that the vice-chieftain could travel in safety) drank a schnapps out in front of the pub, they saw a woman with a very peaceful and satisfied expression on her face as she buried her child in the meadow. She saw the astonishment on Wulf's face and said:

"The way things are today, one has to cry when a baby is born, and praise God's mercy when it dies!"

Suddenly a man came out of the pub. He approached the woman and grabbed her (even though she didn't look as if she could attract a man, for she was barely skin and bones). She defended herself, but the bloke laughed and wanted to wrestle her to the ground. Wulf rode up and lifted the man by his belt, then drove him so forcefully into a blackthorn shrub that the lout couldn't extricate himself at first.

"That was manfully done!" came a voice from behind the farmer. When he turned around, a noblewoman in a lordly carriage nodded to him. "What is your name?" she asked; when he told her she said: "If you're ever in need of a favor, perhaps the countess Trutta von Meereshoffen can open the door for you!" The farmer removed his hat: "Most gracious countess . . . by your word then, an immediate request . . . if I may be so bold. I have a great desire to present a matter of official community business before our exalted sovereign, and without a recommendation it is a difficult thing indeed for a simple farmer, such as myself, to gain an audience with him." The countess laughed: "Report around eleven o'clock . . . you'll get your meeting." She nodded to him, laughed once more and drove onward.

At the stroke of eleven the farmer was in the castle. A lackey demanded: "What do you want?" Wulf looked down at the little man: "By you I will be addressed as 'sir'," he shot back. "I have an appointment with our exalted lord Duke!" The man made a sheepish face and withdrew. Soon another servant arrived and led the Peerhobstler into a room in which an officer of the Royal Guard stood. Several other persons of nobility were already waiting. They all stared at the farmer, who looked like an oak tree towering over paltry juniper shrubs. At first a short old man was called, who quickly returned and whispered to another: "Nice weather today!" Then the officer signaled to the farmer.

Harm felt anxious at first; but when the Duke offered him his hand and asked: "Well, what's pressing against your bunions?" he quickly got to the point as to why he had come. The Duke looked at him earnestly: "Impossible! Or difficult, at the very least. What if everyone complained thusly? Levies have to be paid! What else maintains the roads, or provides for general order?" He knitted his brow: "I want to tell you something . . . but keep it to yourself, hear? In consideration of exceptional circumstances, I will take care of the taxes from my own pocket for five years. But then you'll have to pay, like all the others! By the way, your town's worthy of the honor . . . kept your heads up . . . didn't let your jaws drop like some hang-dog. I've already heard of you . . . that and…," he looked sharply at him, but not unfriendly; "one more thing. Take care that you don't invoke my name unless it's an obvious case of robbery or murder. Understand?" The farmer nodded.

The Duke looked down for a moment, making small talk about the harvest and asking if plague had reached as far as the moors. But then he dropped this in Wulf's lap: "Who are the Warwolves?" The Peerhobstler lifted his hand: "I'm not at liberty to say." The Duke again knitted his brow: "Not even to me?" When no answer was forthcoming, he asked: "You're probably one of them, what?" But then he laughed and said: "Well, perhaps it's better this way. One need not know every-thing . . . less to answer for in the end. I've problems enough already! Hard times, alas! Hopefully things will soon change. Be brave and keep standing your ground!"

As the door closed behind him, Wulf saw nothing but wide eyes. The servant who was escorting him out looked back in a cringingly servile manner, like a robin redbreast preening itself, and tried to ask him questions; but the farmer remained silent and hurried over to the Golden Sun. There he had a quick bite and a beer, then headed out again.

At the door of the pub he met the other Warwolves who had been standing around in twos and threes out front, or sit-

ting within, acting as if one group didn't know the other.
There were still several other men there too, as well as the
bloke who had molested the woman earlier. Wulf now recognized him as the same man who acted suspiciously around
his horse from that earlier time in the Golden Sun with Ul-
father.

The bloke was already drunk, prattling like a jay. As the
farmer walked past the bar, the blow-hard shouted: "Hey
there, you lout! Can't you even bid a 'Good day!' when you
enter a room, as is proper?" The farmer went at him: "Here's
a greeting for you!" and backhanded him across the face so
hard that the fellow's boots wound up where his hat had been
a moment before.

He sprang up immediately: "Dog!" he bellowed. "Dirty
dog of a peasant! You must die!" He pulled his knife, but then
Gustel Gödecke threw a stool at his shins and the man hit the
floor. Ludwig Scheele and Fritz Meinecke grabbed him, took
his pistols, and pummeled him to jelly; they then threw him
out the door so roughly that a cloud of dust flew up when he
landed. He limped over to the stable and got his horse, but as
he tried to mount, Harm took him by the arm: "Beware, you
sneak-thief, beware! There are birch trees and willows a-plenty growing in the moors. This is the second time you've
accosted me. The next time will be the last . . . I'll see to it that
you hang under the Wolf-rune!" He said this very quietly, and
Jasper Hahnebut lost all color in his face, trembling so much
that he could barely get on his horse.

Scheele laughed: "We should have just hung him right
away!" The leader shook his head: "Within the jurisdiction of
the city limits? We'll do well to avoid that sort of thing!"
When Meinecke mentioned: "Well, at least it was a bit of
sport!" Wulf just furrowed his brow and said: "I've had
enough of such sport. Hardly a day goes by anymore when a
man doesn't have to use his fist, or what's in it. And today
especially, I would have preferred to go on my way in peace."

But there was even more to come. As the farmers had ridden for an hour and passed a group of pines, a shot rang out.
Gödecke's black horse reared up and fell over. "Take cover!"
shouted Wulf-farmer, lifting Gödecke (who was unharmed)
behind him. Three more shots were fired, but the bullets did-
n't find their mark. "Let's take nothing for granted!" said
Wulf. "Ride immediately and get as many men as you can,
then we'll smoke these foxes out! These devious dogs! This is
more than just a practical joke. In the meantime I'll watch
where they go."

He secured his horse to a pine and crept along with
Gödecke from the rear, as close to the undergrowth as possible. Both were up to their waist in an old peat bog and peered
out from behind the birch shrubs to the spot where the way-
layers were positioned. It was a dozen Tilly soldiers; they had
made a fire upwind and were turning a skewer over it. Now
and again one would stand, fetch a piece of dry wood, then
throw it on the fire.

An hour must have gone by when Wulf-farmer whispered:
"Head's up, Gustel, soon it'll happen!" Then he hung his lead
billy sap on his wrist and cocked his pistols. Gödecke nodded
and did likewise.

Suddenly the soldiers jumped up, looking wildly about. It
was readily apparent that their mood had changed, for they
ran hither and yon, ducking and looking about like sheep in
a new pen. Harm Wulf heard a robin ticking behind him, and
as he turned around, Thedel stood there grinning widely. The
latter whispered: "We have them in the kettle, all of them
together!" Then he ducked down in a bush, bracing himself
with his left hand.

He had barely settled when a scream suddenly arose: "Holy
Maria!" followed by: "Damned dog's blood treachery!" The
Wulf-farmer laughed between his teeth: "Blood for blood," he
whispered, and looked with fiercely glinting eyes at where the

soldiers were running to and fro. Then something exploded on the other side of the brush, and it once again smelled like smoke. It grew hot as the undergrowth started to burn from top to bottom; the smoke whisked here and there amid the screams that could be heard.

"Hear them chirping, Gustel?" whispered Wulf with a gleam in his eye. Then he raised his pistol, aimed at some shrubbery and fired. Gustel heard a cry from where the shot fell, then saw a man come out of the bushes, engulfed in flames. The latter bolted towards a trench filled with run-off water and landed therein with a squelch.

Shots pierced the undergrowth again and again, one after another, from the right and from the left. Then a voice was heard calling: "Mercy!" But only once. In front of Gödecke something burning crawled out of the bushes, dragged itself over to the bogs and jumped in. The soldier stayed there a moment whimpering, laying in the wet moss and turning around and around. He then tried to climb out, but the farmer didn't let it get that far; Wulf knocked him with his lead billy and the soldier remained still.

"I believe that was the last of them," said Wulf, and Gödecke nodded. There was already a call from behind: Harm Herme, Christoph Otte, and Otto Plesse approached from one side, and on the other Tönnes Hohl, Philip Hasse, and Willem Hornbostel. The seven Fuhrberg farmers' sons were wet like cats and had faces and hands as black as coal stoves; but they laughed boisterously.

"They won't shoot at honest folk again!" said Gustel Gödecke. Harm Herme shook his head: "That's for sure . . . neither will they beat old women to death anymore. They stole a sheep from mother Lüdecke . . . and since she said she had no money, they beat her so that she lay on the ground . . . spitting blood. Blackguards! All of them must have believed her . . . to a man! But now the wolf and the fox need bring no knife to dinner tonight . . . this rabble will be tender enough for them! A shame that there weren't more of them. But let's put out the fires now!"

The work was done quickly, since the fire couldn't spread past the moor trenches; to the right lay sandbanks, on the left was one peat bog after another, and beyond the undergrowth were flat wetlands. "Had they first scouted the area properly," reckoned Christoph Otte, "then probably more than a few might have escaped our grasp. But they were as dumb as sheep when the fires started, and when one ran off in the wrong direction, the others just followed him."

They all laughed, but for the Ödringer Burvogt; he had an annoyed expression on his face. "If things stay this way, we won't get home tonight, Thedel," he grumbled. "That a man's life isn't even safe in the moors and bogs! Now these beastly people roam everywhere, including where one wouldn't suspect. Even with the best of intentions, a man can't ride through the land nowadays without getting his hands red."

And that's how it was indeed. After the fires were doused and the Fuhrbergers rode home, Wulf, Thedel and three others had nearly reached Ödringen; but the cry of the wolf came again from behind them. Thedel answered and two farmers rode up so quickly that sparks flew from the horseshoes hitting the gravel. It was Ludolf Vieken and Schütte.

"There was a dance festival at Tornhop," shouted the Rammlinger, "followed by a slug-fest! Well, it went halfway decently . . . we got early enough wind of it and showed the rabble how we do things here in the heathland." Then he suddenly changed his expression: "Of course the bastards burned the place . . . that beautiful town! And Wieschen Steers, who worked there as a maid . . . she must have recently crossed their path at the wrong moment . . . we found her dead in the bushes . . . everyone else was able to get away and hide."

Harm's half-brother gnashed his teeth and grew purple under the eyes. "It's almost gotten to the point where we

should all just burn our towns down and go hide in the
moors. Yesterday they took two horses and all of my chickens.
What can you do when thirty or forty such blokes show up at
your door? You don't have to fear the odd one or two wanderers that traipse through the heath. Day before yesterday we
encountered three of these vermin in the deep moors. Now I
ask any of you . . . what business would anyone have in the
middle of the wilderness?" He laughed and continued: "Then
our Christian said to them 'Well, since you like it here so
much, then you should stay here!' as he pulled the trigger . . .
and I did too!"

Wulf-farmer had lost his good mood long ago; he made a
face like a brown owl and Thedel himself looked like a hedgehog. "Always, and always again, something comes up!" the latter spat. Harm knew how Thedel felt, because his man wanted to get some grass cut if they got home early enough; but
now it was almost evening.

A bittern bellowed from the marsh reeds; the ducks flew
about; one could hear an owl calling from the wold. The fog
arose from the ground and the sky over the Halloberg Hills
was as red as a girl's skirt.

They rode slowly, and as they approached the outlook,
Thedel gave the wolf-call. "You can be quiet, Thedel!" came
the answer ahead of them, as Christian Bolle emerged from
behind a juniper. "Well! You'll be surprised when you get
home, Wulf-chieftain!" He then laughed: "Some company has
come to visit."

The farmer opened his eyes wide: "Visitors?" The other
nodded: "Yes indeed, man . . . fine company too . . . a visit
from the storks who drink at the Seeben spring!"[42]

"Christian!" shouted the farmer as he bent down from the
saddle deeply. "Christian . . . no kidding? Was it a boy or a
girl?"

42. According to heathland folklore, babies came from the Seebenspring.

Bolle pulled a wide smile: "A boy *and* a girl, Wulf-farmer!
Around four o'clock came the boy . . . an hour later the girl.
And your wife is doing fine, as are the two little ones!"

Harm's expression was like a Whitsun morning. "Thedel,"
he called, "did you hear? Two at once! Boy, looks like I've sur-
passed you. You might have been quicker out of the barn and
. . . well, you have a wife named Hille,[43] too!"

"Yes, but you're a rich farmer!" laughed Thedel. "I only
have my small stead and have to let it grow slowly!"

If Harm were asked afterwards how he arrived at the farm,
he wouldn't have been able to say. "The Devil, I tell you, girl!"
said Thedel as he sat by his wife and watched her breastfeed-
ing their son. "The farmer rode like the Devil! I had to suddenly yell: 'Watch out!' because it seemed like the cuckoo was
going to ride headforemost into the wolf pits!"

As Thedel was telling his story, the Wulf-farmer was
already in the alcove with his arm under his wife's neck and
her hands in his left hand: "My Johanna!" he said, "my good
wife! What a fortune and blessing!" He looked toward the
spot where two . . . three . . . four baby hands appeared on the
bedcovers. He shook his head, then laughed and gave his wife
a kiss on the mouth (but gently, for he saw that her eyes were
again closing). Midwife Duwe waved him off, so he left the
room and went outside, standing before the large doors of the
farmhouse.

He was light in the head. Now he again had two children!
And a woman, so beautiful and clever and good! He looked
over the moors towards the heathland hills where the sky was
yet bright. In the ore bogs a nightingale was knocking about;
the frogs were croaking; the nightjar whistled and flapped its
wings; the air carried the scent of all sorts of flowers.

43. Hille in North German dialect can also mean 'fast' or 'quick', as well as
being a girl's name. Apparently Thedel and his wife already have a child.

He went back inside and ate. Later he went outside again because Gripper and Grabber were growling, but they were only reacting to a wolf that was crying off in the distance of the heath. The farmer suddenly felt peculiar. When he gazed toward the horizon, it seemed to him that the sky beyond the Halloberg hills was growing brighter. But not as if from fire; rather, more as if the sun wanted to rise again. It was extremely red there, and growing ever lighter, with long blue streaks spread throughout.

He shook his head and thought: "What sort of nonsense is this now? Is it a good omen or a dread foreboding?" Then from within the red glow . . . truly and verily . . . he could see it very clearly . . . a great black Wolf-rune formed in the heavens. It remained there for awhile, then dissipated. The red hue alone then still appeared over the hills, and it was beautiful to behold.

He took this for a good omen, meaning that for awhile longer the Wolf-rune would have to stand strong and the Warwolves protect the moors; but then things would clear up, peace would come to the world, and instead of wailing and the gnashing of teeth, jubilation and rejoicing would spread throughout the realm. These were his thoughts as he drifted off to sleep.

For the time being, however, no rejoicing would occur. The wolf cry resounded throughout the heath often enough, and the day scouts rushed here and there more than once. The thirty-three had more work than they wanted, and the hundred-eleven likewise enjoyed few leisure moments. They were truly tired of constantly having to protect the land and guard against mischief. Most of them couldn't even laugh anymore, except for Ludolf Vieken.

But even his laugh was no longer from the heart. One evening he had a pretty girl on his arm, and the very next day he had to stand by and witness her burial. It was but grim satisfaction to him that the dozen and a half Danes who had overrun her home lay stiff and cold under the earth.

Things got worst than ever. As the news spread that Tilly drubbed the Danish king by Lutter on the Barenberg,[44] and was now pursuing the remnants of that army, the fear of him was great throughout the land. But the Danes were even worse than the Imperials; wherever they set foot, they left behind ashes, ruins, and poverty. And no sooner were they gone than the Wallenstein forces followed, raging as if possessed. Reports of peace actually arose, for Tilly was in Celle and dealing with the Duke. But in reality, things got worse; so bad, in fact, that Ludolf Vieken learned an entirely different kind of laugh.

"Drewes!" he said, pounding his fist on the table so hard that the dog started to bark; "for awhile it was actually fun and sport when we went out a-hunting . . . though some might not have thought so. But now it's become a constant chore. We were defensive wolves, but now we must become aggressive wolves . . . and really show our teeth! Wulf-farmer agrees, Drewes . . . nowadays, it's bite first or be bitten! A man can't get a moment's rest anymore . . . it's actually been a week since I've slept in a proper bed! And look at the countryside! Famine and pestilence, pestilence and famine . . . everywhere you look! Whoever doesn't get killed by others thinks about hanging himself or jumping into the marshes to drown. A thunderstorm must come and cleanse the land!"

And Vieken made sure that it thundered at regular intervals throughout the moors. That hotspur had taken the reins in hand, leading the Warwolves from the time that Wulf had remarried; and he did so gladly, for tilling the soil had little purpose anymore. Barely were the oats harvested when a

---

44. Battle of Lutter-am-Barenberg (1626). Tilly, aided by some Wallenstein contingents, deals a crushing defeat to Christian IV and his Danish army.

stranger's horse fed on them, and whoever baked bread was doing it for foreigners. Thus Ludolf Vieken and his men often waited in ambush throughout the moors, and the other district leaders too. Whenever they met up at a pub, then it went thusly: "Well, who has pinched the most lice?" Whoever the best man was, he had to stand a round of drinks for the others.

The men became exactly like wolves themselves, and woe unto him who fell into their hands! If time allowed, then the lead billy was too good, the willow noose too mild; gruesome things were carried out in the wold and moors. One severely cold winter's day, Wulf and his new man, Kasper Schewe, were riding through the heathland and saw some ravens cautiously bobbing up and down above a pine thicket. When then got to that spot, they found four stark naked men tied between the trees. Three were already frozen to death, the fourth one still panting.

Kasper Schewe had been a farmhand in Tornhope, a town which the Danish murdering dogs had burnt down. That was also where Wieschen Steers, who served there as maid, had lost her life, merely because by chance she crossed the path of the firebrands. She had been his sweetheart. Kasper had always been a fellow who said little and only laughed when he had to; but now he said almost nothing and forgot how to laugh altogether, except for those times when he looked after the young heir to the Wulfstead, or the little girl whose name was Rose.

"You should have been a woman!" scolded Mietren, a maid on the farm who was in the habit of saying such things whenever she left the children with him. "What sort of job is this for a man? You play around with the kids while others defend the land!" However Kasper said nothing, as he made a jumping jack puppet dance before the noses of Bartold and Rose.

It clicked and clacked, for he had decorated it from top to bottom with a necklace of pearls and colorful stones that he had found in the pocket of a Wallenstein captain.

"Dumb Trine!" he mumbled, as Miss Mietren's skirt disappeared around the corner; "Dumb Trine!" As he made the puppet dance, he thought about that night he was on duty with Gustel Gödecke and Ludwig Scheele and Bernd Bolle on the main street. "Every day is hunting day, but not necessarily catching day," Ludwig said, as twilight was already approaching. But then he put his ear to the ground. "The deer are bounding off!" he whispered, and made himself ready. Four riders approached at a gallop.

Bernd then pulled on a snare that they had placed across the road. A white cloth suddenly flapped in front of the horses, who startled and stood rampant for a moment. Then three shots were heard, and three times again. Kasper looked on with a dumb expression as his share was counted out: five shiny ducats, a pair of new boots, and all sorts of other stuff, including the colorful necklace that the captain had in his pocket.

"Oh sure, now that it's too late, Wieschen!" he thought; "now we have enough money. What should I do with this junk?" He gave it to the farmer to save, for he needed nothing except food and clothes, and those were cheaply had in the heath (that is, when one knew how to obtain them, and Kasper Schewe knew how well enough). The booty truly meant nothing to him when, from time to time, he along with the others brought down a pair of Danes or Imperial troops, or whatever else there was threatening the district. His only thought was: "There! Now you won't kill anyone else's girlfriend again!" When he played with the children afterwards, he looked like someone who had never heard a shot fired in anger.

He didn't make much of these doings beyond thinking "Work is Work" when he was again on duty. He would have much preferred to do honest farm work or to build wolf traps, for wolves were increasing to a dangerous degree, and the tracks of lynxes were again on the rise. No one was keeping those beasts in check because everyone was busy with worse predators: creatures that had the appearance of men, but were sheer demons who showed themselves more than necessary. The farmers grew wrinkled around the mouth sooner than their years warranted, and many of the sons were as gray at forty as their fathers were at sixty.

Harm Wulf was still a young man, but when his farm was burned, ashes flew to his head and soot in his eyes and smoke in his mouth. When he looked at his beautiful wife and two healthy children, his eyes grew bright again and his lips were not clenched so tight. But his hair was and remained gray on the sides, and rarely did he whistle the Brambleberry Song.

However, one July evening his wife heard him whistling as he returned home. After handing off his sorrel to a farmhand, he went right up and hugged his woman, saying: "Be happy, Johanna . . . peace has come! The Danes are returning home. I heard it in Burgdorf from a reliable source as absolutely true!" The wife made her happiest face, but then put her hand to her breast and grew pale. She quickly recovered though, then laughed and said: "It's the biggest thrill, Harm! Peace! Yes, what everyone has been wishing for! God be praised and thanked!"

It was a lovely evening. The skies over the heathland hills were red, the scent of roses filled the air, and a bird sang beautifully in a niche by the brook. The farmer and his wife sat on a garden bench and gazed out upon the evening. Now and then an owl called from the wold, or a duck clattered by the brook, and young swallows peeped from under the roof. Johanna lay her head on her husband's shoulder and had a face like a church angel. "Peace . . . peace!" she whispered and her eyes grew moist.

But the high nobility didn't get along with each other so well that quickly. Indeed, though the Danes had withdrawn, others remained. Many times yet were the heavens red with something other than the evening sun, and often did the Warwolves have to drop their scythes in the middle of harvest to go and fetch their rifles from the cabinets. The Imperials were still severely oppressing the land, even though the Duke remained loyal to the Emperor (all suspicions to the contrary aside).

Famine and poverty grew to such an extent that the most honest farmer could barely survive except by resorting to robbery and murder. That was the worst of all . . . when the protective brotherhood of Warwolves had to lay violent hands on their own kind . . . people who had formerly only spilled the blood of cows, hogs, and poultry.

It was an April evening when the Wulf-farmer was called out. A report from Meilendorf said that a band of robbers was heading towards the break. They were farmers, from Kalenberg in the Neustadt vicinity and Hildesheim diocese, who had long ago been made homeless. "This business doesn't suit me," said Drewes to Wulf. "Had it been foreigners, then a few more or less wouldn't matter. But these people, driven by hunger . . . it's like when you have to take your best dog out and shoot him for madness. These are folk of our own kind!"

The Peerhobstler nodded: "You know," he said, "it would be best if we gave them a chance to change direction . . . maybe they'll behave reasonably. I'll talk to them . . . I doubt any of them have rifles . . . even if they did, they'd probably fall over from the recoil. None of them have the strength left to wrestle a calf, let alone fight against men. I saw them close up when I was passing by Dietberg . . . the sight made me thoroughly miserable."

The Engenser shook his head: "It's better if I do it. If I get shot, then no big deal . . . my kids are already grown and can take care of themselves ... not yours, though. As senior chieftain, it's more my duty."

The young man Drewes had by his side went and crept among the crooked pines, spreading the news to the Warwolves. "This is pure nonsense," growled Ludolf Vieken. "Drewes is getting old and soon won't be able to lead anymore. I wonder what's going to come of this . . . certainly nothing good!"

And he was right. Barely had Drewes emerged from the bushes and called: "People, I give you good advice! Stay away from here ... the world is big enough!" when a tall man wearing a red woman's skirt as a jacket pulled a pistol and shouted back: "Then make way for us!" and shot the Engenser down.

Almost immediately the shooter and six others lay in the sand, coloring it red. Within a quarter of an hour, two thirds of the band retreated down the path from whence they came, without looking back at those who remained lying in the moors. But that didn't help Drewes; he sat with his back to a juniper shrub, groaning and holding the place on his abdomen where he had been shot.

Wulf examined the wound. "You know something, Drewes," he reckoned, "it would be best if we carried you back to my place. First, it's the smoothest road, so you can lay quietly . . . aside from that, you'll get the best care around, since my wife is skilled in these matters."

Drewes was satisfied, that is, providing his Wieschen would come the next day; he said that he couldn't do without her by his side. And so she came. Harm grew wide-eyed when she arrived, for he hadn't seen her in awhile (though he was often enough near the Drewes farmstead). "She's become a fine specimen of womanhood!" he thought, as she stood before him blushing and paling in turn. "What's wrong with her, then?" he wondered when he noticed, but then gave her no further thought.

Her father was in better condition than it seemed at first.
Wulf's wife soon found the bullet and removed it, but told the
Engenser he couldn't get out of bed for two weeks. "Well, you
won't be bored," she added. "Your Wieschen is here, and when
I have time, I'll read to you."

This pleased Drewes mightily, for lately he had grown
increasingly religious. "Wieschen, come sit with us!" he called,
whenever Johanna came with her Bible. "It wouldn't hurt you
to listen too." But most of the time Wieschen said she had this
or that to do; and when she finally came, she grew strangely
red and white in the face whenever she looked towards the
wife. The latter couldn't make heads nor tails of her, especially since the girl never looked up during meals and struggled
with every mouthful.

Then one early afternoon, Johanna was standing in the living room and watching as Wieschen played with the children
in the garden. The farmer came by and nodded to the girl in
a friendly manner; the wife saw that the girl's face pale, and
then she blushed deeply. Harm laughed as he saw her sitting
there with his children: "You must see to it that you also have
a few of your own soon," he called cheerfully. "I'm surprised
that you're still not spoken for. The Engenser boys must all be
blind!" With that the farmer disappeared around the corner
of the house.

Then a light went on for Johanna. The girl watched the
farmer walk away, looking at him as if he'd done her an injus-
tice; she then wildly kissed the boy on her lap (who was the
spitting image of his father), put her hands to her face and
started crying, so hard that she trembled.

Johanna put her hand to her heart and withdrew from the
window, sitting down on the high-backed stool. She drew a
deep breath and kept clutching at her chest. But then she
stood up, went into the garden, took the girl's hands away
from her eyes and said: "You're starting to get homesick,

aren't you? In three or four days, I think, your father can return." And thereby she stroked the girl's cheeks.

After midday meal she was alone in the house. Drewes slept, Harm and Ul and the farmhand had gone on business, and Mietren was sent out to collect firewood.

"So..." said the wife, as she pulled the girl beside her on the bench, "now the adult women will make themselves comfortable. The children are sleeping like little possums."

The girl blanched and blushed and couldn't look Johanna in the eye. The wife took Wieschen's hand: "It wonders me that a girl such as yourself hasn't got a beau. Don't you like any man? No one can tell me that you don't appeal to them!"

The girl then grew short of breath and didn't know where to keep her eyes; she had trouble swallowing as if something were stuck in her throat. "Wieschen," said the wife, as she put her arm on her shoulder, "I know more than you think. Stay and sit calmly, for we have to speak openly and honestly."

She took the girl's hand and put it on her own bodice: "Can you feel how my heart works so hard?" She drew the girl's head to her chest. "Now you can hear it exactly." Wieschen jumped up and looked anxiously at the woman.

"Yes, girl," she continued. "It pumps wildly, and then sometimes it's as if it stops completely. My twin brother had the same condition . . . in the middle of a good laugh, he fell over and died. And the same will happen with me. Since that time that I had to witness such barbarity, it's gotten worse. Even when I get a slight scare . . . or experience a great joy . . . my heart stops and then starts again, as if it wants to jump through my throat."

She sighed deeply: "There . . . it feels fine again now. But today or tomorrow . . . it won't be much longer . . . it will stop and then..." She held the girl tightly in her arms and continued: "Then my children will have no mother to watch over them. But . . . well..." she paused and dried her eyes. "I know of a girl . . . a good and faithful girl . . . who holds my children dear to her heart. Their father as well . . . and that's why she has, to this day, remained alone . . . though indeed she's the fairest fair and wide."

Wieschen gasped for breath and suddenly fell upon the wife's neck, crying: "Yes . . . but I can't help myself! And it's a sin that I've begrudged him you . . . you, who are three times better for him than me!" She tried to chuckle: "But certainly, your condition can't be that bad! I'll keep my thoughts to myself, then..." she again buried her face against Johanna's breast. "You are so good and . . . he doesn't even notice me!"

The wife smiled: "Wieschen, do you think that a woman who has gone through what I have would kid around about something like this? I've had my share . . . misery and poverty enough . . . and thereafter more fortune and blessing than a woman can expect to experience in these times. If I know that you'll take care of the children, then my final hours will not be unhappy ones. Promise me you will?" The girl nodded, without a word, and the tears streamed down her cheeks.

When the farmer returned, he looked at his wife and the girl, saying: "You two look a sight.... as if you've just taken communion!" The wife chuckled at him, but Wieschen quickly went into the flett.

On the morning of the day that Drewes was to return to Engensen, Johanna sat next to him: "Drewes..." she said as she took his hand (and his eyes, which for a long time had not been as they once were, grew truly ablaze as she looked at him). "Drewes, I want to tell you something now . . . but you're not allowed to interrupt! Listen closely! You yourself told me that you didn't know what to make of Wieschen and her lack of interest in men. Well, since last Friday, I know why that is. All along she's loved someone . . . but one with wife and children . . . and who has thus far looked past her."

She cautioned the Engenser with her finger, for he was starting to make his angriest eyes: "Wait a moment before you start looking askance! The woman of which I speak knows of it . . . and she is happy about it, straight from the heart . . . for she realizes that either today or tomorrow she could die . . . due to her weak heart. And now she couldn't hope for a better step-mother for her children . . . and for her husband..." (here her eyes began to well up) "no better a wife than your Wieschen. Because that woman . . . she is I, Drew-fellow!"

She touched her breast, took a deep breath, and looked at him in a friendly manner: "So . . . now you know it . . . and I think that Wulf-fellow would meet with your approval as a son-in-law. I've already discussed it with Wieschen. Naturally, she still appears somewhat shy . . . but now at least she can look me in the eye, knowing how I feel about her."

Drewes shook his head; he didn't know what to say. Finally he nodded to her: "You could be right, ma'am . . . you're surely right . . . the girl's thoughts are where you say they are. What was for a long time behind bush and undergrowth has now become clear to me. But that other thing . . . that seems unimaginable! You look like Eternal Life itself . . . why, if I were thirty years younger . . . and you were unspoken for . . . then you would see which suitor courted you the hardest!"

He laughed heartily, that is, as best he could. But then he suddenly called out: "Wieschen! Wieschen! Mieken! Mieken!" for Johanna had fallen forward and lay with her head in his lap. As Wieschen arrived, she saw for the first time in her life that her Father, too, could show fear . . . true fear . . . from the expression in his eyes.

The wife soon recovered, and by dinnertime she looked as fresh and healthy as always. But before Drewes climbed into his wagon, he took her by the hand and said: "I will soon return . . . stay healthy!" Then he looked away, for no one needed to see that his eyes had grown moist. However Wieschen hugged Johanna's neck and cried outright, to such an extent that afterwards Harm shook his head and said: "A fine puzzlement of a girl, this Wieschen. At first I thought she couldn't stand the sight of you. Now she acts like she could just eat you up for joy!" He then mounted his black horse and rode behind the wagon with Thedel. The whole time he got not one word out of Wieschen, and didn't know what to make of it.

It was an especially fine day. Towards the evening, as Wulf and Thedel were returning, they heard something . . . as if someone were singing. They stood up in the stirrups and saw a man sitting behind a juniper shrub, holding one knee between his hands and loudly singing: "Gird those, Oh God, with strength in their office, vocation and position, those whom Thy merciful calling has sent to do the preaching work."

The two farmers looked at each other, shaking their heads. When the verse was finished they rode closer, for they saw that they didn't need to make their weapons ready against this man . . . that was as clear as a scorched field! "Good evening," called the farmer. "What on earth are you doing out here?"

The young man nodded, then stood up slowly and replied: "I wish you the same! As to what I'm doing here? Why, I'm waiting to see where the Lord sends me. I'm a preacher . . . although without an official position for some time . . . yet allow that you may formally address me as such."

Thedel Niehus grinned, and the farmer laughed: "No offense meant, Reverend! I could not tell by just looking that thou were a man of the cloth. But where did thou come from, and by what path? Don't take my curiosity the wrong way . . . things are going harshly nowadays in the world.... whoever comes into our district will be asked questions and explain himself!"

The stranger looked him directly in the eye: "Know then, that I am the chaplain Jacob Jeremiah Joseph Puttfarken. Ever since the Lord has allowed the Jebusites[45] to hold sway over the righteous, granting them the Edict Of Restitution,[46] as punishment for our sins, I lost my chaplain's office. Of late, I have been like a leaf . . . one which the wind blows where it will."

The farmer laughed: "Thou does not look much different than a wind-blown leaf, either! But since we were about to have supper, and have more to eat and drink than we need . . . and thou appears to have not eaten to satisfaction today . . . thou are invited to partake with us . . . if thou has a mind to."

The young minister looked towards the heavens: "Lord," he cried, "Your loving kindness protects eternally!" He gave the farmer his hand. "It was yesterday morning . . . in the town of Fuhrberg . . . that I last ate a piece of bread. Since then the bark of the birch tree has been my nourishment . . . though I'm not used to such fare . . . and would have despaired, had I not comforted myself with Scripture . . . He who feeds the young ravens of the air would surely not forsake me."

He ate like a hungry plowman and afterwards already looked healthier, as his pants no longer hung so loosely on the hip. He looked thankfully at the farmers and then asked: "In Fuhrberg I met a relative of a farmer . . . Ludolf Vieken by name . . . born in Rammlingen. I trusted this man, even though he didn't appear to be one walking in the way of the

45. Jebusites refers to an Old Testament Canaanite tribe who controlled Jerusalem (Jebus) until it was captured by King David. Here it means the Imperial Catholic establishment in general, or perhaps specifically the Jesuits, considered the most zealous of the Counter-Reformation forces.

46. Edict of Restitution (1629), a Counter-Reformation proclamation by Emperor Ferdinand II ordering all German lands that had been secularized since the Treaty Of Passau (1552) to be returned to the Roman Catholic Church.

Lord, for all the cursing and unnecessary swearing that came out of his mouth. But the Lord will enlighten him one day! Anyway, he delivered me from the hands of the unholy . . . those who are called 'gypsies' . . . and without being asked, he shared his bread with me, and his beer, when he discovered that my stomach was as empty as that of a newborn babe uttering it's first cry."

He looked upon the farmers with his large bright eyes: "Do you know someone in this vicinity named Harm Wulf? The Rammlinger recommended him to me, for he said perhaps that farmer could use a preacher in his town, whose name escapes me for the moment. Also, that the wife of this man is said to be the daughter of a refugee preacher, such as myself. Or so I was told."

The farmer chuckled: "Did Ludolf Vieken give thou a sign to show?" The other man nodded: "Indeed! Though it seems meager to me, and I nearly tossed it away. Look here!" He pulled a cloth from his pocket and unwrapped a raven's feather which was twice bent, and whose ends were twisted in an odd way.

"That's the right one," said the farmer. "I'm Harm Wulf, Burvogt of Peerhobstel. It could well turn out that thou will find a position with us . . . we men nowadays can barely get to church in another town, traveling being as it is . . . and the women absolutely not. I can tell just by looking that thou are a righteous man. These are bad times . . . and strange wayfarers we generally do not trust a league off . . . therefore thou must pledge before me now a solemn oath, namely: never to betray what thou may hear and see . . . whether thou decide to remain with us or not."

Puttfarken looked at him earnestly: "I have direct experience of that, the sort of thing of which you speak. The three gypsies who threw me down into the street and robbed me now hang in the birch trees. Had the fools known that I

owned nothing beyond the clothes on my back . . . and those
being of a quality that even a Jewish rag merchant would
scarcely accept for free . . . they might be living yet. I've seen
much cruelty in my travels . . . I believe that whoever combats
evil is not going against the laws of God. And so I will swear
what you demand of me."

The farmer waited until twilight; in the meantime, he
asked the preacher everything he wanted to know. This man
suited him, and Thedel as well . . . Gripper no less so!
Therefore he was allowed to sit and ride with Niehus through
the wold and enter Peerhobstel.

"Girl!" said Thedel later to his Hille (who looked as if she
were ready to bear another little Niehus). "We sure raked up
an unusual fellow out of the heath . . . a real odd bird! Sitting
there in the sand amidst his troubles, singing a spiritual song
. . . no knife nor firearm . . . with an expression on his face as
if nothing but angels filled the world . . . even though the day
earlier, he was in the clutches of the gypsies! It's as if he's too
dumb to be afraid of anything . . . he didn't startle one time
when the watches called out to us from their hidden posts."

Thedel was correct. The honorable Puttfarken knew no
fear; leastwise, no fear of Man. Ludolf Vieken got first-hand
experience of it when, four weeks later, he rode up to the new
farm and caught hold of Mietren in the hallway: "Hell's bells,
lass!" he exclaimed, hugging her tightly around the ribs.
"You're filling out quite nicely!"

But what round eyes he made, as the preacher emerged
from the den and said: "The Lord bless your entrance,
Vieken-fellow! But tell me . . . is it necessary to call the Devil's
minions as witness when God allows this maiden to blossom
and thrive? And is it appropriate, in a respectable farmer's
house, for an honest farmer to paw a proper widow's daughter like some slovenly hussy?"

Ludolf Vieken's eyes bugged out, like a hound snorting at an adder. But then he laughed: "Is this the thanks I get for saving thou from the gypsies?"

The preacher nodded: "Yes, and thanks indeed it is! You saved me from the gypsies and heathens, and I will save your soul from hell's fire. So now enter and have a seat until the wife comes . . . the serving girl will call her."

From that day on, the preacher had two fast friends: one was Kasper Schewe, who later said to Thedel: "He really put Vieken-fellow in his place, I tell you! Is that any kind of way to behave? No single girl dares bend over when he's around!" The other was Ludolf Vieken himself, for as he later let slip a swear word, the preacher again gave him what-for. The come-uppance actually amused that devil-may-care rascal as something new. "Hey now!" he said to Wulf-farmer; "Don't let this one get away . . . he's good!"

And that became the opinion of all Peerhobstlers. After Puttfarken was thoroughly fed back to health by the farmer's wife, he really looked like a true preacher. Although still fairly young, he was indeed a good minister, and despite his high-sounding manner of speech, he was a man who could make his way in the world.

He shied away from no work, no matter how hard or far away. More than once Wulf told him: "Thou need not work like a farmhand, now!" But each time the reply came: "Don't you think, Wulf-farmer, that it helps when the people see me digging and lifting just like they are? And besides, it brings me pleasure . . . I myself was born a farmer's son."

He could handle horses as good as any Peerhobstler, and with the passing of time, he also learned to shoot like a seasoned hunter, bringing back many a roast from the wilds. He also knew how to make eel traps, repair nets, and set fishing rods, for he had grown up down south near the Weser river, where his father's stead, along with many others, was burnt to the ground by the Mansfelders.

The farmer considered it no bad piece of business, having collected this man out of the heath. Indeed, alone for the fact that his wife now always had one of her own kind for company when Wulf had to ride overland. And that was often the case. Reports of peace turned out to be no more permanent than the rough frost on the heath, and long forgotten. Things were worse than they had ever been. The Swedes arrived, and the Duke, who had long tired of looking after the interests of the Papists, threw in with them, so that now the Imperials scorched and burned his lands.

The farmer returned home with a knotted brow more often than not, and found it comforting then, when the preacher helped him over his worries with strengthening words and spiritual songs. For Puttfarken had established an evening service on the farm, to which all who had ears to hear were welcomed. Especially the old folks, who hadn't seen a church for years; it was a great comfort that they could again honor God with prayers and song as a community.

Things had formerly gone orderly and sensible on the new farm; but since the preacher arrived, the evenings were even more enjoyable than ever. The young man had all sorts of knowledge and could relate from heart, like a book, all the things that had happened in the world from the time of Adam up until the present. Also, the farmer (in all his years of defending the land) collected every book that fell into his hands, and brought them back because he knew that his wife enjoyed them. So, the preacher read aloud from the best of them during the long winter evenings, and knew how to explain everything so that even Kasper Schewe learned more in one winter than he had during his entire life, up to then.

From the time that Johanna had her own children, she couldn't spend as much time with the others as she used to. Therefore, it came to naturally follow that the preacher held school; at first for the children, then likewise for the hands and the maids. Even the farmers were happy to attend when they could, for anything that took their minds off of the hard times provided them comfort and refreshment indeed.

Yet things still grew increasingly frightening in the world. Even though the town lay off in a remote area, enough reports came that way. When Christian Grönhagen brought a printed flyer around one day, the farmers heard with chilling fear what Tilly and the Papist troops had done to Magdeburg.[47]

The next Sunday there was a sermon service on the new farmstead. Kasper Schewe and Thedel made benches in front of the house out of logs and poles, and in front of the large doors they built a kind of pulpit, which was decorated by the farmer's wife and Mieken with pine branches and posy, and covered by a white cloth with a red cross.

By nine-thirty all of the Peerhobstlers were present, that is, except for the watchmen and the babies. It was a morning that couldn't have been finer: the sun stood bright in the sky; the bush finches argued; the swallows played in the air; roosters crowed from every compost pile.

All the men and women were wearing their finest clothes and had dressed up their children, as best they could. They nudged each other and pointed to the pulpit, whispering softly among themselves; grandmother Horst's eyes grew moist when she saw the red cross on the white sheet.

Harm Wulf started the song: "God on high alone is praised and thanked for mercies given!" and all joined in. During the singing, the preacher stepped up behind the pulpit and prayed to himself. He had on a black robe which the farmer's

---

47. After the battle and during the ensuing sack, the city was engulfed in flame. All of Magdeburg was destroyed and 20,000 of her inhabitants with her. Tilly, who had thought to sustain his army on the supplies within the city, was left master of a wasteland. The loss of this Protestant stronghold caused a panic among the German princes.

wife had made for him, and appeared quite different to the farmers than before, when he went about in his blue work clothes.

When the verses came to an end and the congregation sat down, it was as quiet on the farm as in a real church, save for the peeping of young swallows. "The mercy of our Lord Jesus Christ and the Love of God and the fellowship of the Holy Ghost be with us all," began the minister. He continued with: "Hear with reverence the words of the Holy Scriptures, as it stands written in Psalm 137: 'By the rivers of Babylon, there we sat down and wept when we remembered Zion.'" With that he clapped his book together and started to speak.

The people listened eagerly, for they had never heard such a sermon. It was as if they were talking in conversation with each other . . . so clear and simple . . . and yet so different. He spoke about how things used to be in the moors, and how it now looked here. He resurrected the memory and vision of Ödringen, and let it return again to smoke and ash, recalling in sorrow and misery the deaths, poverty, and all else that the years had brought. All the women cried into their aprons, and the men looked down at the ground in a mournful manner.

The preacher had thus far spoken calmly and evenly. But then lightning and thunder arose from his mouth. With a voice that sounded like a storm, he read from the flyer, hanging words thereupon that came down like an axe upon a tree. "The hand of the Lord will pierce them, those blood-thirsty dogs, who spare not the baby in its crib, nor have mercy upon innocent blood!" he railed. "They shall be crushed by his wrath, and scattered under the feet of their enemies! And when they cry out: 'Lord . . . Oh Lord! Here!' He shall turn a deaf ear, for their iniquities cannot be erased, and their barbarity stands forever!"

The women ceased their crying and the men gazed upon him with gleaming eyes. All faces grew clear as he found comforting words and proverbs to refresh the heart and fill the soul with hope for better days, as well as confidence in the loving kindness of a compassionate God. Everyone there vowed within their hearts to stay the course faithfully, in the fear of the Lord, come what may.

It sounded like a roll of thunder as the congregation recited the Apostle's Creed along with their pastor. And then it rang unto the heavens, indeed, to God Himself, when they sang:

> *That word above all earthly powers,*
> *No thanks to them, abideth;*
> *The Spirit and the gifts are ours,*
> *Through Him Who with us sideth:*
> *Let goods and kindred go,*
> *This mortal life also;*
> *The body they may kill:*
> *God's truth abideth still,*
> *His kingdom is forever!*[48]

---

48. The beloved *Ein Feste Burg* ("A Mighty Fortress Is Our God"), written in 1529 by the founder of Protestantism himself, Martin Luther; translation by Frederick H. Hedge in 1853.

CHAPTER 10

~

Brides and Grooms

The preacher would be right. Half a year later to the day, as the harvest was being gathered in Peerhobstel, the forces of Tilly fell under the scythe of the Swedish king.

It didn't take long for the news to reach the break. Wulf learned of it in Burgdorf, where he had been on business. "Boy, oh boy," said Thedel to Adolf Bolle, "we rode today as if being chased by the Devil himself!"

Three days later they celebrated the harvest festival on the new farm. Never before had the pulpit been so beautifully arrayed with heather wreaths and flowers, and the people hadn't had such light in their eyes ever since they had to leave the old town and live in the moors. It seemed to everyone as if the skies had never been brighter.

And what a sermon they heard that day, like never before! The farmers gazed in awe, for this was something totally different than what the old pastor in Wettmar used to deliver. It was like the fanfare trumpets of a new order, as if an angel of God spoke to them. The only complaint they had about the sermon was that they had to hear it out in the open.

"Tcha," said old man Horstmann, "we've got to have a church, that's for sure! Even if there's no steeple, or if it's built from nothing but crossbeams and bog iron ore . . . it will still be better than hearing the roosters singing along and the dogs yelping in the middle of the sermon. That's my opinion and I'm sticking to it!"

The others agreed and put it before the preacher. "My dear children," he said (and no one grinned to be addressed thusly by the young man), "that was always my heartfelt wish. But I didn't want to add to your burdens. Since you yourselves propose it, I'll only say this . . . may the Lord bless you and your children and children's children, for this great joy that you've given me!"

The building didn't go very quickly because the field work couldn't be left standing; also, more than once the young men had to mount up and ride across the heathland when the horn sounded or the colored staff was passed from town to town, as signal to assemble. Then too, it was no impressive church; rather, more like a chapel. But solid enough were the walls of ore stone, and thick enough the roof of oak beams. And in the wooden bell tower perched upon it was but a very small bell, meant to be heard only by the farms in the immediate vicinity, and no further.

For things grew worse and worse from day to day. From the time that the Duke sided with the Swedes, the Emperor sent one bulldog after another to hound his lands, and there was no end to the deprivation. Up until now, the worst of the storm had passed by the town, but soon it would hit very near. The Papists overran Burgdorf, and five hundred citizens were killed. The survivors were reduced to beggary because whatever money and possessions that were not robbed outright got devoured in the fire. The ashes had barely cooled when the Wallenstein bloodhounds arrived, and the Burgdorfers had to abandon their homes and farms and try to scrounge a living from the wooded wilderness.

The land was filled with horrors, so bad that people despaired of Life, and all culture and manners ceased. The Warwolves didn't hesitate for a moment to take up arms when a large horde of strange, half-starved farmers approached. Thirty marauders were nabbed at once on the Maget Heath and hung on a single large gallows erected over the public thoroughfare; the ringleader got a board across his chest upon which the following was written:

The Warwolves are we,

Three-hundred and thirty-three,

Interlopers, beware our might,

We don't bark first, we just bite!"

This so thoroughly intimidated a band of one hundred people who came that way that they retreated without a second thought. Their leader was nicknamed 'Green Johann' because he dressed from head to foot in green. There was even more blood caked on his hands than on any of those who followed him, and the least of them deserved to be skinned alive from the bottom up.

He tended to swear: "So help me Satan, my dear friend!" And thus he did, as he lay that day in the pine groves with his gang, cursing a blue streak. "A fine gang of outlaws you are!" he insulted them. "Running away from a bunch of hanging dead men! My good friend, the Devil, should take the lot of you!"

But suddenly the pipe fell from his hand, for a voice was heard . . . one that no one recognized from whence it came: "The Devil stands here now, and will take *you* before the sun goes down!" Eerie laughter from the woods followed, so that the women began to squeal like swine and the men jumped up and staggered head-over-heels through the moors.

Wulf and Thedel had to stifle their laughter at the sixty men and forty women, as one old man chased them hither and yon, wherever he wanted. "Yes, I can still do it for fun," said father Ul. "Darn glad that I learned the art of throwing the voice from that crazy Thesel von Rabitze, on that day that he made the people's hair stand on end in the Helmstedt Inn." He lifted his finger: "The horns sound! Well, then . . . until later. An old rag-tag such as myself can't be of any further help to you."

Wulf and Thedel pressed forward in the undergrowth. At four or five positions the horns were sounding, then a shot rang out. The women started screaming as shots fired everywhere. Wulf and Thedel sprang from one juniper to another, shooting and reloading. Harm leapt forward as one of the gang approached; he aimed carefully, his pistol recoiled, and the target turned a cartwheel. The rabble ran together like rabbits in a hutch, getting shot regardless of whether they wore pants or a skirt.

"Lest she breed . . . the vixen strumpet!" said Grönhagen, as he shot a large black-haired woman in the head as she was trying to hide behind Green Johann. Then he jumped the ringleader from behind and pulled him to the ground by his beard. After twisting his arms behind his back, Gustel Gödecke tied his thumbs together. Then they stood him up in front of a pine so he could watch how his murdering gang was destroyed. When it was over, Green Johann himself was hanged before the sun went down, as the Devil had promised.

Though more events than necessary interrupted the progress, the chapel was at last completed, right up to the keystone over the large doors. A cross was chiseled therein, comprised of two overlapping Wolf-runes. The churchyard walls were likewise finished, high and solid, for there were plenty of large stones to be found in the moors. A fence of pointed pikes was erected behind the walls and white hawthorn bushes planted in-between. A trench was also dug all around the walls, deep enough to fill up with ground water. Thus, in times of dire need, the chapel could serve as the last refuge for the farmers.

On the 18th of November in the year 1632, the first grave was dug in the churchyard. As the preacher was performing the memorial service, all eyes filled with tears, including the men's.

For it was Johanna, wife of Harm Wulf, who was being buried. Though she had had her spells now and then, she always looked fresh and blushing, as if nothing were wrong. Only the preacher knew how things truly stood, for she had confided in him.

He looked pale and wretched when he retired to his room that evening and sat by the small iron oil lamp; for his heart, which he had never devoted to any woman, nevertheless always beat more quickly when he but saw Johanna from a distance. Yet by no glance or word did he ever let her notice how he felt. When Mieken came and said: "The mistress has just passed away," he was indeed as white as a wall when he went to the room, his hands trembling as he pressed her eyes closed. No one saw how sadly it affected him.

But on the evening after the funeral, as he placed the church registry on his desk and dipped the goose feather quill in the solid silver inkwell (which one of the gang of Green Johann had in his knapsack), two tears fell onto the rough paper upon which he wrote in his fine large script:

"1632 AD, 18 November, the wife of community leader Harm Wulf, Johanna Maria Elisabeth, born Neugebauer, honored and legitimate daughter of the Bavarian refugee minister Bartold Neugebauer, was here laid to rest. She was a shining example to all women. Lord! Grant her eternal rest and Your ever-lasting light!"

One month later he added:

"She died on the same day that the Swedish king Gustavus Adolphus[49] (God rest his soul!) died near the city of Lutzen."

49. Gustavus Adolphus II (1594-1632) King of Sweden, known as the "Lion Of The North" and "Savior Of The Protestants" for his campaigns during the Thirty Years War, especially Breitenfeld (1631) and Lützen (1632). Breitenfeld is considered a hallmark of Western military history. Had he survived Lützen (in which his mortal wound served to anger rather than dishearten the Swedish army), he might have been able to curtail the war and stabilize Germany.

Again, two tears fell upon the page.

Many a dear hour the preacher sat over this book and wrote, for he asked everything he wanted to know of the farmers concerning what important events occurred in Ödringen and afterwards in Peerhobstel. He had written things down on all sorts of separate notes at first; then (after one particular defensive action) Klaus Rennecke had brought him the book, along with a silver crucifix and a golden altar chalice. All of these things were taken from what the gang of marauders had carried with them. The book was bound in expensive leather and had three silver-plated locks. Now, whenever he had time, the preacher sat down and wrote everything in it that he experienced.

On the first page, a black cross was painted emerging from a red heart, and under it read:

"Our beginning and our end stands in the name of the Lord, creator of the heavens and earth."

On the second page, however:

"The History of Oedringen and Peerhobstel / this is a thoroughly accurate and standing account of the now desolate town of Oedringen and the church and community of Peerhobstel / both, what has come to pass during their times, as well as what had been learned from earlier / for the good and best of posterity and future generations / through J. J. Joseph Puttfarken, minister, 1632 A.D."

Already by the next month, the preacher had to enter another death notice. Although no tears fell from the eyes this time, he did not write as calmly as usual; for again, someone who affected him more than any other in the community was taken.

It was old man Ul. He had had heart trouble for awhile, and when Johanna fainted under his hands and never awoke, he became like a shadow on the wall. Whoever didn't know otherwise would have taken them for father and daughter when they were together. Before he passed away, he had said: "I'm going to visit my daughters, Rose and Johanna."

Three months later, as the first lark was singing over the heathland and the ravens cried out over the wold, the preacher rode to Engensen. He was accompanied by Kasper Schewe (who, in his love for God, served as sexton, in addition to his other duties on the new farm) and Gerhard Mertens (who also became one the preacher's assistants, as one who took no strong drink and spoke no profane word).

Johanna had confided everything to the minister concerning what had been agreed to between her, Wieschen, and father Drewes; she hadn't wanted to burden her husband's mind. The preacher had taken her hand in solemn oath, promising that he would see to it that Wieschen became mistress of the new farm.

"So, this is what the famous chieftain Meine Drewes looks like," thought the preacher as he shook the community leader's hand. He had not imagined him to be so old, with such white hair and so many wrinkles around the eyes and mouth. Although the man stood there like an oak, the worm was within; under the bark it was brittle and rotting.

The preacher knew what was oppressing this man, he who once stated: "Before I allow one finger of me or my family to be harmed, I'd rather walk in blood up to my ankles!" And what man doesn't feel this way, when it comes to home and family?

When the two men were alone (the daughter and maid went out to do the milking), the preacher then began discussing Wieschen and the Wulf-farmer. Afterwards, the old man made it plain what was foremost on his mind, and the preacher comforted him as best he could. "Whoever protects himself and his own kind against oppression and cruelty, and defends widows and orphans, Drew-fellow", he said, "our

Lord God will call that one 'welcome', though his hands be
red upon red." With that the old man sighed deeply and said:
"Then I won't worry so much about it anymore, Reverend."

Later, the preacher discussed things with Wieschen. The
more he spoke, the less she did. Finally she said: "I thought
that I had accepted it . . . but that's not so. I'll keep my word .
. . I would do so even if in the meantime I had become smit-
ten with another. That hasn't happened, mind you! Even
though Harm has no thoughts for me . . . and it would be
dreadful if he thought that I lurked in wait for the death of his
wife. Every time I went to church, I prayed that God should
give her a long life. Since the day she talked it out with me,
I've been as fond of her as a sister. And if Harm finds someone else he prefers . . . and she's good to the children . . . then
I would be happy. For all the world, I wouldn't have him
thinking that I want to force him . . . just because his blessed
wife once had a wish."

The preacher gave her his hand: "Such is an answer befitting a Christian maiden. Leave yourself in my hands. My dear
friend Harm will think no ill of you. And now I'll be happy to
hold a small evening service at the request of your father, for
it will soon be time to prepare for departure."

During the service he noticed a girl kneeling next to the
daughter of the house, with a face that reminded him of his
late blessed mother. She had the appearance of one who had
suffered much, but when she once looked up at him, he felt
that her heart had remained pure and good. Afterwards he
learned that she was the maid. He didn't understand why he
was fixated upon her, as she put the chairs to one side. He
would have gladly known more about her situation, but did-
n't dare ask at this time.

Twilight had come as he rode through the heath with the
others: the fog arose from the ground; the frogs were croaking in the ponds; a wolf howled at the moon from the wold;
cranes were boasting from the marshes. The skies were red in

the vicinity of Meilendorf; a farm, perhaps an entire town, was burning. The preacher prayed quietly to himself: "Save them, Lord, from the wicked. Shelter them from the sinful!" They were almost at Brehloh when suddenly a couple of crows clashed loudly in the trees. "Whoa!" cried Gerhard Mertens, pulling back on the reins of his horse. The others did likewise and took pistols in hand. At that same moment a red flash came from the bushes, and a bullet flew past the preacher. He immediately shot back and heard a man scream. Then he saw that another man was taking aim at his sexton; he rode over quickly and knocked him into a heap. When he turned about, he heard a bang; the fellow who had been trying to get up fell over as Gerhard Mertens shot him.

When they reached the clear heath, the preacher stopped: "Let us thank the Lord for His goodness," he said as he removed his cap. "Let us pray . . . Lord, Lord, my mighty relief, you shield my head in times of struggle." As he redonned his cap he said: "It stands written: 'Whoever sheds the blood of another, his blood will likewise be spilled'. It doesn't stain us . . . whoever lies in ambush for his brother's life, such a one is like a wolf . . . whoever slays him is not besmirched by his blood. Our hands are clean before the Lord!"

The next day Thedel, Klaus Rennecke, and Gerhard Mertens came back near Brehloh and searched for the dead bushwhackers. The wolves had picked the bodies clean, leaving behind only a handful of thalers and a pair of good pistols. "I must say," Thedel mentioned later to Wulf, "that's the sort of preacher who fits us well. I thought he could only shoot with quill and ink! Goes to show, one doesn't truly know about a man until he's eaten three bushels of salt with him. I'll just say "Our Preacher!" Such a man is a real find. Who would have thought it, that day we found him singing behind the juniper shrubs?"

After the ambush, Puttfarken stood even higher in the eyes of the community. And since he took it upon himself to man the watch in his turn, without being asked, he himself did not have to ask for the house that was built for him across from the chapel, as was befitting. Also, all that belonged in a house appeared of its own accord. "Now the only thing lacking is a good woman," said Wulf, "then thou would be set!" But Puttfarken shrugged and looked down, saying: "There's time enough for that, Wulf-fellow." As he sat over his books in the evening, though, his thoughts often wandered towards the maid from the Drewes farm.

The next day, when he met the farmer (who was busy making trenches) and took supper with him, he began: "Wulf, yesterday you mentioned that my house lacked a woman . . . and I said that there was time enough for that. But now I want to tell you.... your house also lacks a woman. Let me finish! I don't say this because I think you're ready to forget your blessed wife . . . or that your eyes are roving towards another . . . I know you too well! But it's mostly on account of the children . . . also, because you may not realize that there's a girl who has liked you from the first time she saw you . . . someone who would be the best step-mother for your children that one could imagine."

The farmer at first shook his head when the preacher mentioned it. But when the latter explained that Johanna had confided in him, and asked him to see to it that Wieschen kept her promise, Wulf could only reply: "That young beautiful woman is much too dear for the likes of me. Look here!" (and thereby he removed his hat) "I'm half gray already . . . I've had to shoulder all sorts of burdens over the years . . . the best that I have to offer is half-buried in Ödringen under the ashes . . . and the other half buried under the lawn by the church. That girl deserves a man who can offer her more than I can."

The preacher said no more about the matter for the moment. But after other visits to Engensen, he kept bringing up the subject, and didn't let it go until the farmer said: "When a year has gone by since my Johanna has passed on . . . and if Wieschen is still of a mind to do what she told thou . . . then so it shall be, as she promised my dear wife. For the children's sake it would be best if she came tomorrow . . . but that would be against custom . . . and besides, I won't touch a woman until a year has passed. I didn't wait that long after I lost my first wife . . . I've often enough regretted it . . . even though it couldn't have gone differently."

A week later Wieschen arrived. However she did not come alone; her father accompanied her. The preacher made it clear to Drewes that the two young folks should get together and henceforth care for one another, the sooner the better. To that the old man replied: "And me? Nobody thinks about me! What will come of me when Wieschen leaves? Lieschen has her husband and children and no time for me. If I'm included in the bargain, then I'll agree . . . otherwise, no deal!"

He had, however, his ulterior motive when he said that. Although he would have indeed missed his daughter, his main concern was that he wanted to be near the preacher; for whenever he looked into that man's eyes, he then forgot the dumb thoughts that so haunted him of late. He didn't see the many white faces with red holes in the forehead, didn't dread the men, who hung by willow nooses from the birches, swaying back and forth, that came into his vision whenever he saw a birch tree or a clock pendulum.

"That suits me fine!" said the preacher, who suspected what was on the old man's mind. "And if you don't like it on the new farm, you are heartily welcome to stay at my house. I'm all alone . . . like a badger in his hole . . . and I certainly can't hang around the Wulfstead all evening, every evening."

But Wulf wasn't having any of that; he framed out the big bedroom for Wieschen and Drewes. The girl and Harm lived under the same roof, but as brother and sister; the betrothal and promise of marriage became settled in early July. And although, according to ancient custom, they were already considered married by their relatives, the bridal suite was crossed only after the preacher had performed the rites; as matchmaker, he insisted upon that courtesy.

"Understand," he said to Harm, "I myself am a farmer's son, and know well that engagement and living together counts as full marriage, even before the vows are taken at church. But those vows will be taken when the year is up, as it should be. Firstly, so that you two start out with a fully lawful and proper Christian marriage . . . especially in your position, where there is already an heir to the farm. Secondly, because a Burvogt should set the example in these things to the community. Lastly, because you're no bachelor, impatiently awaiting his wedding night." The preacher was highly pleased as the farmer immediately shook hands on the deal and said: "That is my opinion entirely."

It was only a quiet wedding; the groom was not in a dancing and drinking mood, and the bride especially not. Additionally, Duke Christian had recently died and there was mourning throughout the land. And when it came right down to it, these were no times for celebration. But the preacher held a nice ceremony nonetheless, and many of the townspeople remarked: "In a way, a wedding such as this is indeed more appropriate . . . rather than one ending in raucous eating and drinking bouts."

The bride was very quiet the whole day before, and looked as white as chalk during the ceremony. She was overly concerned that the farmer felt compelled to take her. The next day, however, she looked her usual self; for when she was alone with her man that night, he took her hand and said: "In the time that you've been here, I've indeed discovered that I'm not as old and cold inside as I feared. I haven't shown how I feel about you these past few months because I vowed not to touch you until the day we were married. But now, Wieschen," (he thereby hugged her and gave her a kiss) "you are my wife! And to the best of my powers, I promise you'll never regret it."

With that the young woman cried so forcefully at first that the farmer grew anxious. But when he moved her hands from her face, he saw that it was a sun shower, and his wife then laughed and threw her arms around his neck.

It was also a good thing that Wulf's wedding had but a small toast around the table afterwards, because the very next morning, half of the Peerhobst Hill young men were called to arms. Renegade gangs of Swedish soldiers were seen in the vicinity, starting to create havoc. Since their king had died, they had lost much of their discipline; molesting women and mistreating children had become mere sport to them. But when one gang tried to march through the moorlands, they soon learned that gnats swarmed around those parts in winter too. As they laboriously slogged through the snow and morass with their work horses, the leaden gnats started to bite so hard that the blood ran. "Tcha," said Ludolf Vieken, "those unfamiliar with local customs often end up looking stupid."

By Epiphany Sunday the Peerhobstlers again sang: "and though this world with devils be filled!"[50] That was indeed the case, for nothing but news of murder and arson came to their ears. Once, an entire week went by without a red glow in the skies (beyond that of sundown), and the people felt almost as if they had missed something. Another corpse lying in the streets wasn't even noticed, no more than a dead cat. The preacher was hard-pressed to the task of keeping his community true to the word and teachings of Christ; like disease on the body, these gruesome times weakened the soul.

---

50. The beginning of the third verse of Luther's "A Might Fortress Is Our God."

His heart nearly stopped in his chest when he was told of the ways that the farmers took revenge upon their tormentors. He was quite taken aback when Kasper Schewe told him, in all calmness: "In Brelingen, a tenant farmer who lives in the woods has kept a Pappenheim soldier prisoner in a pigpen on a chain for six months, so that he has to eat from a trough. The farmer is right! Those swine raped his wife, and whoever acts like a pig should live like a pig."

Today the Imperial troops, tomorrow the Swedish soldiers . . . things grew increasingly perilous. One day it was: "Wienhausen has been plundered!" and the next day, "In Old Celle the pastor was beaten to death!" The longer it continued, the worse it got. The meadows were lousy with freebooters and laggards. "If things continue like this," grumbled Schütte, "we'll soon run out of willow limbs for nooses and will have to plant new trees ourselves!" But Ludolf Vieken laughed: "We won't have to go through that much trouble! Before it comes to that, the birches will all be hanging full, as unpleasant a sight as that might be for any length of time. Anyway, the lead billy works much quicker."

Things turned extremely grim when Duke George, brother to the sovereign, went back over to the Emperor; the Swedes had treated him like a peasant. Now it was as if hell had disgorged all of its devils at once. The pastor no longer commented when he heard about how the farmers were paying back like with like. Tilling of the land had all but stopped; stable and sty stood empty; people dug after wild roots and ate mice and rats, snails and frogs, dogs and cats. Sometimes the meat that went into the pot or onto the spit was not even from an animal, either domesticated or wild game. A few unfortunate souls who had gone but one hundred steps from their town did return . . . but in pieces, and carried under the coat. Parents had to stay keenly vigilant if they wanted to keep their children.

The pastor was not even thirty years old, but already gray-ing at the temples, and the creases around his mouth were as deep as those that old men bore. All things considered, life was still tolerable on Peerhobst Hill. Even if the harvest was poor, and each house had to bake tree bark or acorns into the bread, they were always able to fill their plates; in the wilder-ness there were always all sorts of things to eat, and never a lack of game or fish. But the worst thing for the people was that they were under constant fear that one day soldiers would find their way to the town, in numbers so strong that the community wouldn't be able to defend itself.

The preacher himself felt ill at ease under the collar. Not that he was afraid for himself; rather, he hadn't been able to sleep peacefully at night since that time that the Croatians wreaked fair havoc near Engensen. Granted, they had had to immediately retreat, for the Warwolves outnumbered them three to one, and none of the camp-follower rabble found their way back. Nevertheless, he couldn't stop thinking what might happen in such instances to Grete Thormann, the maid who served at the Drewes farmstead.

He had immediately noticed that the girl suffered a trau-matic experience in her past, and he asked old man Drewes about it. She was the youngest daughter of the Tornstead, which her parents abandoned when a band of marauders overran it. That was when Wieschen Steers, Kasper Schewe's sweetheart, came to her terrible end. The farm went up in flames, so then Thormann moved to another farm in Wettmar that he owned (and which had been rented out). However, eight weeks later the whole family was dead, save Grete; she survived only because she was in service at the Drewes farm. She was taken in there then, and treated like a daughter, because Witte Drewes, the head of the clan, was her cousin.

"What I'd like to know is, why our preacher always goes back and forth to Engensen?" said Thedel to his Hille, who in the meantime already had a fourth child at her breast, and thereby grew ever rounder. "Not a week goes by that he doesn't ride there." His wife laughed: "He probably has business up there with someone in a red skirt, and who wears her hair in a bun, I reckon." Thedel replied: "Him? He thinks about everything but women! Naw . . . this time you're off the mark, girl."

But it was indeed as Hille reckoned. Before another month passed, Grete Thormann moved onto the new farm with all her worldly possessions, which were not many. From then on, the preacher spent more time there than at his own house. The following Sunday he read the banns for himself and Grete from the altar, and two weeks later they were married by the pastor in Wettmar in a quiet ceremony.

After that, the preacher no longer looked so somber, and his wife also wore a new expression; especially ten months later, when she acquired new duties in addition to baking bread and milking cows. After two months, she had grown so round as to make her skirt rise a bit higher above her heels from the back, and the preacher himself gained like a gander that gleaned the overflow from grain bins.

The best wedding tale, however, was provided by one Kasper Schewe. He had always squabbled with Mietren, and the two couldn't stay out of each other's way. At any given moment one might hear Mietren's voice: "Boorish lout! Dunderheaded jackass!" or something along those lines; the grumbling response would be: "Dumb Trine! Ol' blabbermouth!" Finally Wulf's wife had a noseful; when she heard them bellowing in the cowshed one day, she slammed the doors, slid the wooden crossbar lock, and shouted: "So! Now stay in there until you can get along and become friends!"

Now, since the rear wall of the shed was only interlaced slats, the farmer's wife crept back there to eavesdrop. "Harm," she said that evening, laughing so hard that the bed squeaked, "it's a shame you weren't there to hear it too! At first everything was quiet. Then Mietren started in: 'Get along? With such a repulsive creature? I don't even think about it! Such a stand-offish dog! I care what he thinks of me about as much as a rooster can carry on his tail! I'd rather seek another position. That's all I need! Who was here first? He should go back to where he came from!' Suddenly she changed her tone and said: 'For what did I always sew his slippers and darn his socks and patch his pants? This is the thanks I get?!' Then she started crying loudly. After a moment, well . . . she stopped crying, and I heard Kasper grunting like an old badger. Then all was quiet again, so I opened the doors. When they came out, Mietren averted her eyes and walked past me quickly . . . but Kasper was grinning like a honeycake horse. Then he said to me: "Many thanks to you, ma'am. We're going to be married in four weeks!"

And so they were. After eight months a little Kasper and tiny Mietren arrived, and Kasper Schewe was suddenly at no loss for words. Also, he remembered again how to laugh.

"Reverend, I'm sure I don't know what's happening nowadays," said the Wulf-farmer. "It's like some sort of Divine plan. Wherever one looks, it's raining twins . . . that is, when it's not triplets! If this continues, then our children will have to build a church five times as large, and put far more land under the plow than we do now! Wieschen brings me another pair to go with the first . . . thy dear wife hasn't held back . . . Bolle has had four children in two years . . . and now Kasper Schewe hasn't been shabby either! It wasn't like this in former times. Well, when I retire and pass on the colored staff and large horn, the leader who follows me will have twice the work!"

And it wasn't just that way on Peerhobst Hill. It was as if folks, through double and triple births, were trying to fill in the holes that war, pestilence, and famine had torn . . . and

kept tearing. Entire towns were abandoned, others had barely a quarter of their original population. Whatever didn't die
wound up scavenging around the wilderness, or lay half-
starved outside the walls of Celle (where at least the cannons
provided some security against the couriers of death that
were unleashed upon the land by the Emperor today, the
Swede tomorrow, with absolutely no end in sight). Ten years
and more they'd been playing the role of Land Scourge. When
the children who grew up during these years were told that
there was once a time in which people pushed away from the
table with a full belly each and every day, they just laughed
and said: "What a tall tale!" These times were so horrific that
people ate the corpses of those who died of disease, and parents killed their children rather than watch them starve to
death.

Farmer Wulf told the preacher of the gruesome things he
had experienced on a recent trip to Celle. The legislative
assembly gave Duke August the means by which his brother,
George Iron-hand, could wage war against all enemies of the
state and outlaws. Appraisal upon appraisal was levied, and
even farmhands and maids were taxed to their last coin. That
was why Wulf rode to the city. Countess Meershoffen, whose
hair had already turned gray (her three brothers had been
devoured by the war, and outside the gates of Lüneburg, her
sister and those attending her were killed in a grisly manner),
gave him a letter so that he would be allowed an audience
with the State Minister.

The Minister met with the farmer for an hour, then
accompanied him to the Duke. Wulf related to the latter how
he and the other Peerhobstlers had been fending for themselves. The Minister already knew the half of it from rumors
and reports. The Duke, who was somewhat more of a timid
sort, paled when the farmer told him: "Most Excellent Lord,
although we didn't keep count, it could very well be that we've

stretched several thousand necks." But the Minister said: "Ach! If only there were more towns like yours . . . if only! Then things would stand far better for our poor nation." The Minister spoke awhile longer with the Duke, in confidence. Then he told Wulf: "His Excellency declares the Peerhobstlers relieved of their tax levies for the duration of the war, in recognition of their forthright bravery and proven loyalty."

Two days later, the farmer returned to Celle with twelve of the thirty-three under-captains. He placed a sack with one thousand thalers in gold on the table, as a freely-given gift to the state. "Just a little something we scrounged together during our campaigns," he said, "and I believe our Lord Duke may have a use for it." The Minister pounded him on the shoulder and shook his hand. "Burvogt, you're a hale fellow, well-met! By the will of God, I wish we had more of your kind! How long will you be staying in Celle, and where are you quartered?" When the farmer told him, he tossed back: "In two hours I'll be sending something your way."

Within the hour, a lordly carriage pulled up to the Golden Sun, and a chamberlain with an attendant stepped out. They went into a room reserved for the nobility; soon the innkeeper emerged and waved to the farmer: "Your presence is requested!"

The chamberlain unrolled a scroll and read what was upon it. The farmer's head nearly started to spin, for it was far greater than he expected: tax relief for Peerhobstel for the duration of the war, official recognition of the parish of Peerhobstel under the stewardship of Pastor Puttfarken, exemption of the new farm from all liens and burdens for all eternity, with the exception of provision of a mounted soldier during times of war.

"Your honor, this is too much," said the farmer; "Too much!" But the chamberlain smiled, then took the case that his attendant was holding. He opened it and said (while showing the small picture in the gold frame, upon which the face of the Duke, as he lived and breathed, appeared): "Our most gracious lord sends you this token of his thanks, along with the message: should you ever have another request, don't hesitate to ask."

The preacher was happiest of all when, that same evening, the Wulf-chieftain sent around the colored staff and called for a town feast. He couldn't contain himself, and had to run straight home and shout to his wife: "The Duke has officially recognized the parish, Margarete! And me too! Thus, we can stay here until the Lord calls us to Him!" And thereby the tears ran over his face and he had to sit down, as his legs grew weak for a moment.

The preacher truly needed this joy, for it constantly weighed upon him how the war threw its shadow over Peerhobstel, making the people hard and cold. However, now he had the text for the following Sunday. He would make it known to the congregation how good they had things, compared to what other people had to suffer. Thus, they shouldn't moan and despair; rather, live in the fear of the Lord and hold their heads high.

The people shuddered that Sunday when they heard about what was happening in other places, and thanked God that their town wasn't faring like some others in the vicinity. For the preacher had read to the congregation from the flyer that Wulf had brought back from Celle, which ended thusly:

> *Two children, who had been driven*
> *From their home and farm,*
> *Were found in the woods,*
> *Starving and freezing.*
> *In their hunger, they had been*
> *Gnawing on their mother's heart.*

~

CHAPTER 11

The Imperials

It was a hard winter, and the snow remained on the ground for a long time. The Peerhobstlers were afraid that their footprints would lead enemies to them, and so after every snowfall they had to make false trails throughout the heathland that led away from the town.

At least they had something to occupy their time and prevent them from falling into melancholy from boredom. To keep activity going, as soon as the cold waned for awhile and the ground softened, Wulf-farmer started to build a solid log cabin within the walled fortress. There was always a chance that the worst could happen, he thought, and another gang of marauders find their way to Peerhobst Hill.

Thedel immediately followed suit, and then Bolle and Henke and Duwe and Rennecke. In the end, everyone wanted a lodge with shed within the fort. They built the cabins close to the wall and covered them in sod so that they wouldn't easily catch fire. To make things even more secure, they made the trench around the fortress deeper and steeper, then diverted a spring towards it.

After that, the access path was dug away and replaced with a drawbridge. Also, a well was dug. Finally, all the powder and lead that could be spared was stored in the lodges, along with extra firearms and other weapons; also pots and pans, firewood, clothing, provisions of all kinds and livestock fodder, as well as all the beehives from the town. When everything was finished, Wulf called a town meeting and announced: "Now let the enemy come, if he has the heart. We'll give him what-for!"

The farmers held their heads higher. What more could happen now? If the foe approached, let him try his worst! There was plenty of wood in the wold; all sorts of possessions and cash were secured in the walls; before an enemy could even get near the town, the watches will have already spotted and reported him. After the harvest, watch patrols were out-fitted even better than in the summer. The outposts in the trees were made so solid and secure that it was easily tolera-ble for the watchmen in the winter, since there was no lack of clothing and pelts (the Warwolves had seized plenty of those). In addition, mounted scouts rode through the heathland all day long.

The preacher saw to it that the evening hours didn't hang heavy on the people; he provided all sorts of ways for them to occupy their time. In the vicarage he held get-togethers in which the Holy Scriptures would be read, and on many days he read from other books, so that the people could once again enjoy a hearty laugh. He told them how it looked in the marshes near the lower Weser river, where he had been raised, and what he had experienced in university. Also, one after another of the villagers would likewise give their tongues some exercise and talk about this or that.

Even Kasper Schewe took his turn, and was very proud that everyone laughed so heartily—though they did so because not a one of them could make head nor tail of what he was saying!

Every two weeks a dance was held on the new farm for the young folks; Fritz Witte knew how to bow the fiddle and Hinrich Duwe played an excellent flute. Things were merry on dance evening; lively but sensible, since no more than one beer was allowed. And even if the shrieks were few, and the red skirts did not fly so high as in former times, there was neither quarreling nor fights, and no hangovers the following morning. The married folks danced too, and a great cheer arose when even the preacher showed that he and his wife could take the floor and match the best of them; when it was ladies' choice, all the girls wanted a turn with him. "Yes, our preacher . . . he's really something!" said Thedel as he headed home with his Hille.

Thus the winter passed, sooner than one would have thought, and without bringing any unusual inconveniences. Mind you, once a large band of Swedes came fairly close to the town and were spotted when Wulf and his two farmhands were on guard duty. Kasper Schewe then showed that he wasn't as dumb as he acted, performing a deed that made him a famous man, even to his wife, who never let a day pass without chiding him for his introverted demeanor.

Sitting in the pub at Engensen eight days later,Schewe swelled in pride when Ludolf Vieken said to him: "If you weren't a married man, we'd probably make you chieftain. But now, tell us again how it went!"

"Tcha," started Kasper, "that was the morning after the night . . . tcha, the very same morning that Duwe's white-headed cow gave birth to a two-headed calf. Tcha, I thought immediately that it was a sign, I thought. Tcha, and so it was. By eight o'clock . . . maybe it was nine . . . the farmer said to me and Gerhard: 'Let's head into the heath a bit, just for a change of scenery'. Well, then we ride! Tcha, and when we were almost at the Bulls' Moors . . . I mean, we were still by the Hoeltke springs . . . and what do you think? Here comes a rider with forty more following! 'Gerhard', said the farmer then, 'head quickly for Peerhobst Hill and sound the alarm! We have to see to it that we get help.' Tcha, and then I got the idea . . . honest and truly . . . and I say: 'Wulf-fellow,' I say . . .

'if we now ride in the undergrowth upwind, and I make sounds like a cow or two or three, and like a calf, and I could squeal like a pig too . . . tcha, I can . . . maybe we can draw them away from the road.' And the farmer was satisfied with that. 'Kasper,' he said, 'now that's an idea!' Well, so we go into the bushes until we're upwind . . . and then I let loose . . . at first softly: 'meh . . . meh...' like a calf. And then 'moo . . . moo...' always louder until I'm bellowing . . . and in between 'nawf, nawf, nawf,' and 'swee, swee, swee...' just like a pig . . . and now and then I let out a whinny like a mare or a foal. Tcha, and what do you think? They really fell for it, those dumb-heads! And we drew them out of the Bulls' Moors towards Osterhol . . . and from there towards the Nienwold . . . and from there towards Duesterbrook . . . and from there to the wilds of Neegenbarken. And then we took off . . . you never saw such riding! Clippety-clop, clippety-clop . . . to Rammlingen to call for help. Tcha, and the rest, well . . . you all know it better than I do!"

That was actually quite amusing. There happened to be eighty of the three-hundred and thirty together in Rammlingen. As the two Peerhobstlers arrived with their report, Schütte called out: "That's fine with us! And now I'll tell you all, let's do it differently this time. That same old lying in wait in the bushes has gotten boring, I say. Let's gather another twenty men or more and then ride straight for them. There'll be the Devil to pay if we don't trample them under-foot!"

Wulf had a different opinion; but all the others were in favor of the plan, thus they headed out. On the way they picked up another thirty men, so now they were one hundred and ten strong. They blackened their faces and rode forth. Gustel Gödecke and two others rode to the front and took point.

The Swedes were moving through a desolate place called Valley Of Tears, where there was nothing but sand and crooked pines. As the soldiers reached the middle of the moor hills, the farmers fell upon them from two sides. The young men blew their horns and cracked their long whips. The Swedes had a bunch of stolen horses which bolted furiously upon hearing the whooping and snapping, running over each other and breaking away in all directions. Then the pistol, truncheon, and axe did their duty . . . not stopping until the last rider was out of the saddle. But seven men of the Warwolves were also wounded, the worst of all Schütte; he was shot through the chest and died a quarter of an hour later. He last words were: "Boy, that was some sport!"

A large pit lay in the middle of the Valley Of Tears; all the Swedish troops were thrown therein, and since then the place has been called 'Swede's Gap'.

Not far from there lay a swamp, which came to be called 'Where The Big Dogs Bite'. In February, another troop of Swedes were encamped there, fifteen strong; the farmers were getting ready to head over and clear them out of the way when Thedel and Gerhard rode up and reported that a dozen Imperial troops were approaching from the other side. So Wulf-chieftain said: "Well then, let the dogs bite each other!" He rode to the town, got dressed like an Imperial, and then rode past the Swedes, making sure they got an eyeful of his colors. They pursued him immediately, but were poorly skilled at riding through the high heath. Wulf lead them into the midst of the Imperials, then made himself scarce. As the Imperials and Swedes went at it hammer and tongs, the farmers enjoyed this theatre from the wings; afterwards, they moved in and swept the chaff from the hill.

That provided enough topic of conversation back in town until the Spring arrived, and one had to wonder where the time had gone. The war continued to rage, but tilling of the fields began and the people again had a purpose. They still had to hide in the moors like wolves, for each day soldiers passed by, hither and yon; and too, the black death was again making the rounds. Therefore the Peerhobstlers kept to themselves, so as not to carry the pestilence into the break. They were accustomed to keeping their houses clean, didn't suffer from hunger, and lived in moderation; therefore the epidemic might indeed have eyed the town, but decided to pass it by.

The people overcame their fears and worries in the best way possible: through work. Thereby they had little time to care about what went on in the world outside of their village. "I don't know anymore . . . are we on the side of the Swedes or the Imperials?" asked Burvogt Wulf of the preacher. Ludolf Vieken said "The Regent himself doesn't know which way to lean . . . that's why he allied with the Hessians and goes against all who don't belong here . . . exactly like us . . . that's the best and only way!"

In the meantime Harm had grown very gray; chasing up and down through the heathland (and all that went with the task) had taken the color from his hair, made his brow stern, and his mouth narrow. Otherwise he was still at the age where twelve hours in the saddle were no great hindrance. In all important matters he was now again the chieftain, for Ludolf Vieken was too much of a hot-blood and impatient in tactics. Were it not for Wulf, that Rammlinger would have long ago been under the earth. One time (when he yet again had an itchy trigger finger) he came across four Swedish riders; they had Vieken covered, to the point that it was pretty much over for him. One of them was about to run him through with a sword as he sat in his saddle, but then the Peerhobstler came thundering over and broke the soldier's neck. He then lopped the arm off of another, and gave a third one a gash across the forehead; but the forth one managed to put his saber through Wulf's cheek before the latter knocked him into the ground. "It's only a flesh wound, old girl," he said, as he roundly patted his wife on her bottom. "Bind me a cloth around it and fetch me a piece of honey bread . . . then I'll stop whining."

The farmer's wife could laugh then. Wieschen had also aged somewhat from these hard times, but was nonetheless lovelier than ever. She remained the prettiest women far and wide, and the liveliest and merriest too (which was even more important to the farmer, who often had his dark and somber moods).

Wulf was becoming like Drewes, who now played the grandfather. His daughter had her fourth child by this time, and when the old chieftain chased around with his grandchildren, he could still laugh so that all his teeth showed. But when he slept, he often saw the many white faces with red holes in their foreheads, and birch trees full of dead people swaying back and forth like the pendulum on a clock. Then he'd have to go and talk with the preacher, to dispel those troubling images.

Such thoughts haunted his son-in-law as well; yet most of his worries were still about the future. For eighteen long years he had had to play the wolf, and he waded through even more human blood than Drewes. But even if it flowed up to his neck, he would not have thought much of it . . . if only he could finally see the end of it all!

But the heathland was still wriggling and crawling, lousy with untrustworthy folk: Swedes and French, Croats and Slovaks, and all sorts of mixed rabble, eating what the farmers grew and what their wives milked. Robbery and Plunder . . . Torching and Burning . . . Abuse and Oppression . . . Murder and Torture . . . there was no end to it!

And so sometimes the farmer thought: "It might have been better not to defend ourselves . . . then we'd be in the ground and our troubles over!" But so long as the horns blew and the hammer-board chimes resounded, complaining of strange dogs in the road . . . he reached for the firearm in the cabinet, took the lead billy sap from the antler rack, and threw his legs over the black horse. And when he returned the next day . . . hungry, tired, wet from rain and sweat, and reeking like a horseherd from pine, myrtle, and heath . . . he then said after all (laughing a little thereby): "This time we knocked them off the mountain!" He would then fall upon his bed and sleep the entire day, like a dead man. The next day, however, he'd wash from top to bottom, put on clean clothes, play with the children and take his wife in arm. Looking at him then, one could not imagine that this was the same man who two days earlier, when asked by an imperial officer for mercy, replied: "Indeed . . . but of this sort!" and thereby struck him dead.

And what else was he supposed to do? Whether Swede or Imperial . . . either cooking with the one or brewing with the other . . . in one place people were tortured to death in the name of Holy Mary . . . and elsewhere flayed for the sake of the pure faith.

In addition to all the current woes, George Iron-hand was killed by poison that he allegedly got in Hildesheim when he met with the Swedish general; now it looked like the land would be engulfed in blood. The farmers of most districts could finally no longer stand the oppression, so they banded together and helped each other the best they could. And if things didn't work out for them, well . . . then that wasn't bad either, because whoever was dead no longer needed to have their heart broken over this torture-filled existence.

Ludolf Vieken had cried like an overrun dog when he heard the news that two-hundred farmers were killed by the Imperial troops at Dachtmissen; he had a friend there, and also something else still dearer to him. He rode forth with his people, but got there too late, and only managed to encounter twenty of the soldiers. Six were taken alive, one of them an officer. They were all dragged into the wilds and hanged like common criminals. When the captain protested, Vieken shouted: "Then treat this 'gentleman' like an officer, and hang him with his saber belt instead of a willow noose!" Indeed, some say he had earlier spat in the captain's face.

That must have been true, for almost immediately thereafter his punishment came:[51] he had to marry! As to how it arrived: he should have kept his fingers off of Gustel Gödecke's sister Trina, for in most things the Warwolves could tolerate sport and kidding, but not in such matters. So he let his face hang like a roebuck in want of a doe, as one evening Gustel said: "Our Trina reckons that it's about time for you two to get married." The wedding was two weeks later, and a merry one it was! Merry, that is, for all but the groom; he was overheard mentioning to Christian Grönhagen: "Yes, the women . . . a man has to be careful, for they immediately take everything you say to heart, word for word!"

Afterwards he remained second-in-command, and was happy when outside matters occupied his time. "This constant smooching!" he moaned; "Good heavens, climbing only makes sense and reason so long as the apple remains on the tree . . . afterwards, it's mere nuisance!"

Thus he and his brown horse were often on the road, for each day it rained vermin whose sole intent was to pick the land clean: today the Swede, tomorrow the Weimaraner, day after that the Hessian . . . and then it all started over again. However, he enjoyed this life; when he returned home and threw a handful of thalers on the table, with a couple of gold pieces in between, he'd say: "If this continues, Trina, you're going to have to knit your money sock right up to the top of your thigh!"

But one time, when he came home and told her (in a very joking manner) that now a man should take two wives . . . even three . . . because war and pestilence had swallowed too many men, so that one-to-one was no longer practical, well . . . Trina made a pair of eyes like a cat caught in a chimney, paid off Lotte Wesseman (her maid, a single girl) on the spot,

51. Perhaps some sort of superstition about upper/lower class interaction or violation of military protocol?

and then took as servant another woman, one who had the appearance of a scarecrow. He said to Grönhagen afterwards: "A porcupine is as smooth as a child's hand, compared to my Trina. Oh well . . . the hard to reach fruit always tastes best!" But he didn't get much chance to dwell on these regrets. Today the Imperial Colonel Heister came a-struggling, tomorrow Torstenson[52] and his Swedes went a-fiddling about the countryside. Farmers with wives and children languished outside of Celle, starving and waiting for death, debating which tasted better: an Imperial sirloin or a Swedish rib-eye. For things had degenerated to the point that human meat was eaten openly, and conspiratorial parties of manhunters often set out. The Peerhobstlers, however, didn't need to resort to such things. They still had all sorts of livestock and wild game a-plenty; although occasionally they would eat horse, if a bullet mistakenly found mount rather than rider during a campaign in the heathland. Then they'd opine: "Ach, well . . . mare's veal tastes good too!"

One morning in May all three captains, Drewes, Wulf, and Vieken, were sitting on a bench in the garden of the new farm. The peonies were in bloom, the swallows flew back and forth, the bees were going about their business and the children sang:

> "May-beetle soar,
> Dad's off to war,
> Mom's in Pom-er-a-ni-aw,[53]
> That duchy's burned forevermore,
> May-beetle soar!"

52. Lennart Torstenson (1603–51) commander of victorious Swedish forces at the second battle of Breitenfeld (1642) and Jankau (1645), the last gathering of any significant Imperial army.

53. Pomerania, a region in northeast Germany on the Baltic, part of which is now Poland.

They sang and laughed and squealed and jumped after the bugs, whose wings looked like gold as they flew past the sun.

"That's a new song," said the Engenser, "not one we sang as kids. Yes, each day the world is new." The Peerhobstler nodded: "But not better, Drewes . . . I don't believe that I'll live long enough to see peace." The Rammlinger chimed in: "I'm of the same mind. Up until recently, I thought it was all great sport. But now . . . I don't know . . . maybe it's because one gets older . . . or maybe because I now have little children. Anyway, I'm losing my taste for sneaking around and fighting. After all . . . it's just too much, when day after day one has to take the lead billy down off the peg."

One of the watches in the heath sounded his horn, then another; and a hammer-board chime was heard, then another. Harm and Ludolf arose: "Well, no use complaining . . . the work has to be done. Adieu, Drew-fellow . . . I'm curious as to what the ruckus is now! The hell of it all is, my Trina doesn't believe that, when I'm laying around outside, I'm only in wait for the Swedes and such. Each and every time it goes: "Well . . . the Swede again! He's probably wearing a red skirt . . . and I wouldn't be surprised if his name was Lotte!" He scratched behind his ear: "Oh, yes . . . the women! They're awful cute for the most part . . . if only they didn't have such sharp tongues!"

He let loose with a sigh that was as long as an arm. But Drewes laughed: "That serves you right, Vieken-fellow! That suits you fine, you cock-hound! If you had a wife like other men, people would feel sorry for her. But on a stone pot goes a stone lid . . . that's the natural order of things . . . like with like . . . the squirrel doesn't mate with the toad! But now get going, before we get flea-bitten!"

And get going they did. The watches had been keenly vigilant and the wood chimes held long resonance. The Imperials made dumb faces when the tooting and blowing and ringing started on all sides; and then even more so, as shots rang out from unseen men, for the woods were thick and the marshes wet. They were more than happy to beat a retreat to the open heath, double-time, because between the crooked pines and junipers, horses heads with human faces above them soon appeared here and there, and always more, like when the woodpecker starts hovering around a beehive.

"There are more than one hundred men," said the officer who had put his ear to the ground; "The Devil knows where they're all coming from. Forward, march!" Thus the Imperial troops withdrew, with heads and faces following their every step. The farmers rode behind them . . . here three . . . there ten . . . another two yonder . . . and a few more all over the place.

"They'll come up short of breath today . . . and it'll cost them some horsemeat, too!" laughed Wulf. Ludolf Vieken suddenly galloped to the fore until he was about one hundred paces behind the soldiers. He then stood up in his stirrups, looked over the juniper bush, cracked his whip and shouted: "Hyah! Hyah! All aheaaad! Strike deaaad! All dead, all dead, all dead!"

It was as if a hornet's nest had been dropped into a crowd. The officer cursed and hit two men in the head with his saber so that they fell to the ground, but there was no holding the Warwolves off; from front and from back, from right and from left, everywhere the cries "Hyah!" and the cracking of whips and the dreadful war whoops. Then the officer shrieked as he threw both arms into the air: "Blessed Mary!" He tried to retreat, but the lead sap of the chieftain found his neck. At first he merely leaned forward in the saddle, but as his dappled caught a hoof in a water hole, he fell dead to the ground.

"Well, how did it go?" asked Drewes, when Wulf and Ludolf returned in the afternoon, wet as frogs and hungry as threshers. "Fine!" called out the Rammlinger. "They took to their heels and will still be running by tomorrow. We gave them a good reason to high-step, something extremely persuasive. They won't soon return . . . there are about twenty others that we have to go track down . . . probably go back no later than midnight. Man, do I have a hunger and thirst! Mistress Wulf . . . a worker deserves his wage, and threshing the fields stretches out a man's stomach. But you can't watch me today, when I kneel behind the ham, Wieschen . . . otherwise you'll think that my Trina doesn't feed me!"

Drewes-father laughed, remembering how often he too came home from such outings, hungry enough to butcher a hog. "Boy," he said as he filled the stoneware stein to the brim, "a man gets a new lease on life listening to you boast! And that's exactly how it is! A sporting good time . . . even if afterwards a man's mood grows dark when he's lying in bed. Ah, well . . . it's only right . . . and we've shown that we're no meek lambs . . . so let's drink to that: everyone raise a stein to not getting skinned alive!"

He passed around the stone mug on which was inscribed, "Vive! Long Live Friendship!" But when he tried to hand it to his son-in-law, he had to first nudge him, for Harm was looking over to the garden where the children were playing a new game, and singing thereby:

"The Swedish have come,
Now everything's gone,
Smashed windows all 'round,
Dug lead from the ground,
Poured bullets so hot,
Now everything's shot,
Evvvverrrything's shot!"

CHAPTER 12

~

The Swedes

What the children sang was soon to become reality. The
Swede came; fear preceded him, misery followed him,
and pestilence walked alongside.

"Pray, children, pray!
The Swede will come today!
Tomorrow Ossenstern[54] will reach you,
Praying he will gladly teach you!"

With such a song one put the children to bed; they learned
it and sang it just as energetically as the May beetle and lady-
bug learn to fly, so that it brought a chill down the spines of
their parents.

Everywhere reports of peace were discussed, but no one
believed that it would come to that; not even when
Oxenstierna[55] took up residence in Celle, and then traveled
from there to Osnabrück (where the other dignitaries were
getting ready to hold the realm's wake). One would sooner

---

54. This refers to Count Axel Oxenstierna, Gustavus Adolphus' most senior
nobleman and the person instrumental in advancing Sweden's power in the
Baltic. When Gustavus Adolphus died in 1632, Oxenstierna effectively took
over the running of the campaigns in Germany during this phase of the
Thirty Years War.

55. This was John, son of Count Axel, who represented Sweden in
Osnabrück at negotiations of what would become the Treaty of Westphalia,
officially ending the Thirty Years War.

believe in the end of the world, and everywhere people were running about, shouting: "Fear God and pray to His Glory, for the time of His Judgment has arrived!"

The preacher himself grew disheartened and said to his wife: "Margarete, it's hard not to doubt God when one hears how things are. Farmer Vieken told me that the Swedes are torturing children for amusement. On the recent baggage train that he captured, there were eight young girls harnessed as pack-carriers, the Swedes whipping them with cords as if they were beasts. Indeed, and that was the least of what they had to endure. God . . . my God . . . why dost Thou allow such things!"

He had it very rough, for the farmers were muttering against the Lord. "What's the use of being good," said Kasper Schewe, "when nothing comes from it except fears and worries?" But he fell silent indeed when the pastor scolded: "For shame, Kaspar! You, who have healthy children, a lovely wife, and enough to eat each day!"

Still, that thought of the farmhand occurred even to the minister and Wulf, and all others alike. Even the Rammlinger arrived one day and said: "I've had a noseful, up to here! All I want to do is walk behind the plow and come home in the evening to play with the kids . . . not go out every couple of days to kill men!"

As time went on he had accustomed himself to his Trina, especially since a baby girl soon followed his firstborn son; as the saying goes, a skirt-chaser (such as he once was) often turns over a new leaf from the joy of having a girl of his own. Whenever he had time nowadays, he went around with the children. And he was no match for his Trina. She caught him once with a serving girl in his arms and cursed him out dreadfully, shouting: "Just one more time and I'll jump into the marshes . . . and take the little ones with me!" This put the fear of God into him; he swore high and dear that his days of youthful folly were behind him, that he would now behave like a husband. As far as his own farm and village knew, he kept his word. But he traveled often, and there was a scarcity of men in most towns, thus he was hard-pressed to keep his promise.

One fine May morning he was riding through the Bulls' Moors with one of the wildest of the younger Warwolves, Helmke Schierhorn. He was as happy as a lark, for he had just enjoyed a very pleasant visit with an old friend, one Lotte Weesemann. "A fine day today, Helmke!" he said as he lit his pipe. He puffed contentedly as he looked out over the heath. "Helmke, look! Two strange riders . . . Swedes or something. Let's go on over and wish them a good day! What do you think? 'Always polite' said the crow, bowing each time he stole an egg from the peewit!"

Schierhorn was in full accord. They hung their leather billy saps on their wrists and pulled their pistols, then rode towards the riders under good cover. The first horseman was shot out of his saddle by the Rammlinger, but then he suddenly noticed that it wasn't two, rather a whole dozen Swedes before them. Now it was time to make like a rabbit and push their nags to the limit. Indeed, two shots followed them, but did no damage beyond taking half the tail off of Helmke's dappled gray. As they had nearly gained the woods, they were confronted by ten more Swedes, and thus had no choice but to head into the undergrowth for cover.

The Swedes searched for awhile, but then withdrew. On the road they met two gypsy women and learned from them that there was a town deep in the wold. "Beastly folk back there live, fine Lord!" said the old one, and the young one added: "They make all dead, what is good people, soldier 'n gypsy!" The sergeant of the watch said: "Ah, so there's where that lot hides! Well, we'll smoke 'em out!" He took the women with him and rode straight away to Fahrberg, where Count

Königsmark[56] was camped with many men, and made his report. In the middle of the night one hundred and fifty men were dispatched to camp in the Maget Heath until dawn.

It was still quite gray when Gerhard heard them approaching; he was on watch by the Bulls' Moors with Adolf Bolle. He blew his horn, but then he heard the alarm sounding likewise by Kohlen Hills, and then by the thorn trenches as well; the Swedes had approached on three sides simultaneously! The Peerhobstlers were barely able to get themselves and their livestock behind the walled fortress. Wulf entered second-to-last, with Kasper Schewe staggering in after him; the latter had gone back and quickly retrieved the portrait of the Duke from the living room, as well as a yellow-colored cat. "So the children have something to play with in the meantime," he said.

The Swedes stalked into the town, sharply on their guard. Everything was quiet but for the cackling of hens and the twittering of swallows. The soldiers approached the houses with weapons in hand; no people could be found. They looked into the sheds and cellars, but everything was empty. The eerie stillness put them on edge. But then a rider came running up with a Swedish coat that he had found on the Horstmann farm. After a thorough follow-up search, many weapons and clothes were discovered which obviously belonged to Swedish soldiers who had been shot dead. "If I have to search forever and three days," cursed the captain, "I'll find these people, and then you men can have some fun with them!" The soldiers laughed; but it was guarded mirth, not fully heartfelt.

It took three hours, but the outer ring of the fortress surrounding walls was discovered; eleven soldiers died immediately when they fell into the wolf pits. The rest arrived in one

---

56. Swedish general Hans Christoph Königsmark, notorious for allowing his troops to pillage during the closing phases of the Thirty Years War; occupied Prague in 1648.

piece, but couldn't see through the house-high thorn shrubs that were solidly interwoven around the fort. "Two men, to the trees! Report what's on the other side!" commanded their leader. Two men climbed the trees, but no sooner had they reached the tops, and were about to open their mouths, when two shots rang out; they both fell to earth like full sacks.

"Those swine!" cursed the captain. "Make a breach in the shrubs!" The soldiers started pulling the briars away, but the work went slowly because they had to break it apart piece by piece, so thickly were the thorn bushes bunched together. They suddenly stopped, for horns sounded from within the walls; it was sinister to hear, like when wildcats start to whine and wolves cry in answer. It immediately started to resound likewise on three sides. The soldiers looked around nervously, not especially pleased by these events.

"Well? Let's go!" shouted the officer, and he started whipping the backs of the men who were clearing the briars, so that it cracked loudly. "Thirty men . . . front and center . . . On the double!" The soldiers worked noisily. A raven flew over the wall, cawed loudly, then circled back. A black woodpecker chortled as the jays complained about the racket. "Quickly, quickly!" shouted the captain; "We'll have them within the hour! Let's show these bushwhackers what it means to shoot God-fearing Swedish soldiers like roebucks. Onward! The sooner we're finished here, the sooner you can return to your girlfriends!"

Ludolf Vieken laughed: "Or perhaps not!" he said through his teeth, with a sideways glance towards Wulf. The latter was in no mood for jokes: "You traipse around with your women," he said, "and now our backs are also exposed. What a disgrace! I always knew the day would come when your antics would put us in a fine soup. Well . . . no use squawking about it now, though. Now the important thing is: no unnecessary bullet . . . no inch of skin exposed . . . and everything done as

I say! And whoever doesn't follow his orders will get what he deserves afterwards!"

Ludolf Vieken felt a shudder as he saw Wulf standing there, weapon in fist, red in the face and blue under the eyes, with a mouth in a thin grim line. But then he recovered when his leader ordered: "See to it that the beehives are in place! And the women are to boil pitch and water. But return quickly! Wait . . . give all the young boys weapons too . . . today everybody lends a hand, with head and neck at stake . . . and even more than that . . . because if they get us, they'll kill us slowly."

The thorn hedges were now penetrated to the point where the faces of some of the soldiers were visible. Ludolf Vieken aimed, but Wulf quietly growled: "Are you mad? We've got to make the head fall first, then the body will follow!" He looked through the shooting slot peep hole in the wall, then stepped back and pushed his rifle through, aimed steadily and fired. A bellow arose from across the hedge. "He won't be barking orders so loudly now," he whispered to the Rammlinger. "Right in the chest! Took off like a weasel." He jabbed one of the youngsters: "You boys are to toot and ring out as loud as you can . . . we've got to get help, understand? Even if the blood shoots out of your ears, I better keep hearing you, or you'll hear it from me!"

The Swedes stood around their captain. He lay in the grass with his back against a pine; each time he took a breath, bright blood spurted from his chest. A very young officer, still nearly a boy, knelt beside him and wiped the death-sweat from his forehead. The dying man moved his lips; the young man bent over, then nodded and jumped up: "We must avenge our captain! Volunteers to the fore!" But only a dozen stepped up, foremost the old sergeant of the guard. "Pack of louts!" gasped the officer. "By the women you're heroes, but here you make in your pants!" He pointed at particular men who were trying to duck to the rear. "You there . . . forward!

And woe to whoever takes a step in retreat!" He held his pistol up in front of his eyes.

The men grumbled. They were indeed manslayers of the worst kind, but this eerie fort . . . in the middle of wet marshes . . . stocked with sharpshooters . . . not to mention the strange tooting and ringing going on all around . . . it all made their throats clench. The officer called twenty by name: "I'll count to three, and whoever doesn't charge the moat will be swallowing his own blood. Think of Gustavus Adolphus! Think of Breitenfeld! You're the Swedish army, not some band of rag-tag renegades! So . . . everyone take two pistols in hand and dagger in teeth. For God and Sweden! One . . . two . . . three!" He grabbed his chest and fell into the grass; Wulf had shot him through his heart.

The sergeant threw a fast glance back at his dead captain, then shouted "Forward . . . March!" and leapt down into the moat. Suddenly the trench was filled with Swedes. But it was as if the water were boiling, for they all screamed horribly as one; they had jumped at the spot where sharp spikes were below the surface.

"Shoot them dead, at least . . . this is frightening!" cried the preacher. But Wulf-leader shook his head: "No, Reverend . . . we can't spare the time nor the bullets . . . and the longer they squeal there, the more the others will hold back. But go now . . . check that the watches are sharp and that the alarms continue to sound from all sides . . . then tend thou to the women and children . . . they need you more!"

Suddenly it again grew still. One could hear the finches squabbling and titmice peeping; now and then a cow would bellow from the stalls. It seemed at first as if the Swedes had departed. But after awhile the banging of tools could be heard. "Make ready the bees!" said Wulf to Kasper. "The boiling water and the tar, too! They're probably making a bridge. Well . . . I doubt that will be of much help to them . . . nevertheless, let's stay alert!"

Harm breakfasted but kept his eyes on the peep hole all the while, and then lit a pipe. He had gotten past his aggravation over the Rammlinger. Besides, the watches had reported that replies to their alarms were coming from two sides, and so he thought: "Things will turn out all right after all!"

But then he chided himself for an oversight. He should have had a bullet-proof watchtower erected within the fortress, for then he could have seen what was going on beyond the outer hedge. "Well, the eyes are always keenest in hindsight," he thought.

He sat thusly for two hours; then the chopping and hammering ceased. One could hear the soldiers dragging and groaning. Wulf ordered the men: "Make yourself bee-proof and fetch the hives! Then man the shooting slots around the entire wall, and here…" he turned towards Ludolf Vieken, "the sharpshooters take position here . . . but don't shoot until I say . . . not even if I shoot first!"

Soon there stood twenty bogeymen to his right and left. The farmers had donned bee masks, wrapped towels around their necks, and put on thick jackets and three pairs of pants, tied off at the bottom. All had thick gloves on, their firearms standing before them. Behind the leader and Vieken lay the beehives; they were tied to long poles, humming within like teakettles, for the hive exits were blocked.

The Fuhrberger whispered: "I have an open shot!" The leader nodded: "Then fire!" A shot rang out, followed by a scream from the other side, then a loud curse. One could hear the thorn bushes crackling. A bridge of pine poles bored its way through and crossed over the water, slowly at first, then at a quicker pace. Harm turned his rifle to the side, aimed and fired. Another curse arose from the other side. "Whoever has an open target, shoot to kill!" he ordered. "But be careful . . . we have no men to spare!" Five shots rang out and the bridge fell into the water; but it was lifted again when a high and broad shield wall, made of fir limbs and pine branches, appeared.

"Who wants to throw the bees?" asked Wulf. "No married fellow . . . you neither, Ludolf.[57] But Helmke, you!" Schierhorn stepped over to his captain. "So," the latter ordered, "when I give the word, you six there open the hives and pass the poles to Helmke as fast as you can . . . you others give him covering fire so that no one can stop him. And if he falls, Hinrich takes his place . . . then you, Jochen. But under no circumstances throw the hives into the water! All of them have to go into the thorns. We'll handle the people on the bridge soon enough!"

A mare within the fort neighed, and a stallion answered from across the hedge. One could hear tooting and ringing in the distance over the heathland, and those in the fortress answered back. The cuckoo called, and a yellow butterfly flew over the water, alit on the head of one of the dead men, then continued on over the thorn bushes. "He's going to go get the others," whispered the Rammlinger, and grinned.

No sound could be heard from across the moat. Then the bushes rustled, and suddenly the bridge shot across the water, embedding itself into the wall. "Be alert, and shoot calmly!" whispered the leader. Six Swedes bolted across the bridge wildly. A few shots rang out from the fort and only one of the soldiers made it across, a young man with hair as light as a child's. "Don't shoot!" called Wulf. "Take him alive!" Thus, as the young man tried to clamber across the porch, Shierhorn dragged him up and over, throwing him towards Vieken. "Tie him up and lay him down . . . but don't harm him!" ordered their captain, as he shot once more across the moat, then shouted: "The bees!"

---

57. A little barb at his friend, who obviously was a married man, but whose recent indiscretion led to the current mess they were in.

Schierhorn, who looked like Satan incarnate with his mask, heavy clothes and the lead truncheon on his wrist, ducked down by the protective wall and peered over. A hand grabbed onto the wall and the farmer gave it a good whack with his sap; a scream arose, the hand disappeared, and there was a splash in the water, followed by a long shriek. Another shot was fired and the water splashed again.

As if he did this all the time, Kasper Schewe stood calmly behind the Ehrlershauser, reached for a beehive, ripped open the bottom, grabbed the pole, then passed it to the hands of Schierhorn. The latter took the hive, swung it forward and then yelled "Look out below!" as he discarded the pole and reached for another; then a third and a fourth . . . then the fifth and the sixth.

Swedes were again running across the bridge. Three were shot and four climbed onto the porch, but Schierhorn and Kasper threw them back into the moat. Suddenly curses and cries could be heard from beyond the hedges, along with a great buzzing and humming. There was no end to the swearing and yelling; it grew ever worse, and one could hear how horses were fighting against their binds and tearing free, how hounds were yelping, and how the humming grew ever more severe. The air was alive with bees. Behind the wall, Ludolf Vieken was doubled over in laughter, slapping his thighs so hard that it resounded smartly as he called out: "I'm dying here . . . I'm dying!"

Wulf had to laugh too. Then he went over and cut the bonds of the Swede and said: "On your feet!" The young man stood there, chalk-white in the face. The farmer grabbed him by the collar: "Do you speak German?" The youth trembled over his entire body: "Yes," his voice cracked. "You're German yourself?" The soldier nodded. "From where?" demanded Wulf. The boy choked: "From Saxony!" The farmer took a deep breath: "Blackguard! Actually I should kill you now, trai-

tor! But run over to your people and tell them to retreat. We
still have plenty of bees, and our friends will be arriving soon.
And if someone asks where you were, tell them: 'In the hands
of the Warwolves!' You're the first that we've ever let go alive."
The soldier shook so severely that he was barely able to get
across the bridge; when he got to the bank on the other side,
he fell over.

Wulf held up his hand: "Hush! I hear the horns again.
What's going on? That's our people! Listen . . . they're shooting! Boy, what luck . . . I was just getting thirsty!" He drank the
entire stein of thin beer that one of the men handed him, then
he said: "Now we've got to see to it that our bees calm down.
They'll be plenty aggravated, and probably all confused, too!
Someone run now and tell the women the news . . . but they
shouldn't come out yet! Not if they want to keep their pretty
faces . . . the bees will swell their cheeks like orangutans. Half
of you can now go and see what mother has cooked for us . .
. and leave some over for me!"

He listened towards the wold and nodded. More and more
shots were being fired, and the tooting and blowing never
stopped. The farmer stood there, tall as a tree. Then he
laughed: "Hear that, Ludolf?" The latter nodded: "Our boys
are putting a lead billy salve on those Swedish bee sting blisters . . . best thing for it!" The leader raised a finger: "Our men
have them surrounded on two sides. Quiet! Hear that? Boy oh
boy, what a shame we're not out there!" He twitched in excite-
ment: "Listen how they bellow: Strike deaad . . . Strike deaad
. . . All dead, all dead, all dead!"

And then a song arose from the log huts; the two farmers
listened as the women and children sang out: "Now thank
God, all of ye, with heart and voice and hand!"

It didn't take long for the Warwolves to arrive. They
laughed and called out over the moat: "Hey there! Looks like
you boys had matters well in hand. We could have stayed

home! So, first let's get rid of this dumb thing and chop it up for kindling!" Wulf-farmer shouted: "No! We can use it in here . . . bring it over by the drawbridge! But first let someone come on over and tell us everything that happened . . . we're curious as the devil, you can imagine!"

Jasper Winkelmann from Fuhrberg and Hinnerk Ehlers from Engensen crossed the bridge. "Boy oh boy," said the Fuhrberger as he pounded the Rammlinger on the shoulder, "I see you've dressed up in your best finery! Going out to call on a lady, are you? Anyway, it's a shame you fellows weren't with us . . . we could barely shoot for all the laughing! I reckon none of them will ever eat another piece of honey bread again. You should have seen how the horses bolted . . . and the soldiers . . . man, I tell you . . . we were rolling! They yelped like young pups . . . I'd bet that behind every juniper in the heath there's someone itching the stings in their hides. Never laughed so hard!"

Wulf took off his mask: "Usually it goes: 'First work, then play'," he said, "but here on Peerhobst Hill, it's just the opposite with us. Call a few men up with nails and rope and axes . . . we want to quickly make a tower, so that if they return, we can greet them from above. In the long run, beehives are too dear . . . and what will the children say about this squandering of honey?"

~

But the Swedes didn't come back; neither those nor others. What no man thought possible appeared to have come true. Throughout the heathland word spread that, indeed, honestly and absolutely, peace was to be declared. One could see it in various signs: storks again nested on housetops and not just in the wilds; winter crows flew south earlier than usual; the population of mice (and the damage they cause) receded;

as did the gelatinous globs which folks call "star sniffles"; no fiery men shone in the heavens; birds of pestilence and death no longer flew about, as if blown away by the winds.

Bands of marauders and their camp followers still moved about the land, but their best days were past. Wherever they let themselves be seen, the townspeople joined together and smote them; the same with gypsies and whatever else built no solid hearth and home. The farmers emerged slowly from the wilds and again hung their kettle hooks on the hearth (that is, if their homes were still standing) or built new houses as best they could. Here and there, plows again cut furrows into the earth and fields were planted. The dead were again being given a proper funeral, and no longer buried in an old sack.

But the peace was not trusted entirely. After all, it was unthinkable! Peace? To work and eat and sleep without fear and anxiety? No more red glow on the horizon from towns burning? No alarums or cries of pain to be heard? To be allowed to sing and laugh again? And to play and dance? And to be happy when a baby is born? Whoever believes that is naive, or the war has distorted his reason! It's time to keep an eye on that one! War could soon erupt again! We've seen it before! After the Peace of Lübeck in 1629, things got even worse! And that's already been sixteen . . . no seventeen years ago. And four years earlier, didn't the Duke make his peace with the Emperor? And what good was that? None at all . . . it all flared up again, even worse than before!

But people finally were convinced as things truly changed in the world. Poverty and distress were always present, of course; but murder and torture were no longer the norm. Also, flowers bloomed in much greater numbers, the birds never sang more cheerfully, and the air was very different, no longer filled with the smell of smoke and blood. So what the preacher reported in the chapel must be true after all: the Emperor and the princes were serious about it this time.

Otherwise old Drewes wouldn't be holding his head so high again. "I just want to live long enough to see it with my own eyes . . . then my time here is done," he said.

And live to see it he did. It was the beginning of November when Ludolf Vieken came wildly riding up, shouting like a demon. He jumped from his horse like a youngster and spun the farmer's wife around in the air so that her knees showed, laughing as if mad, then said: "You probably think I'm drunk, eh? Not a drop! I'm as sober as on the day I was born. But it's peace, I tell you . . . peace for ever, surely and absolutely! If you don't believe me, read this . . . or let the preacher read it aloud! I bought it from a man who brought a bunch of flyers like it from Celle. It has the seal of our Duke on it! There, Reverend!" He fell upon the bench panting and suddenly the tears poured from his eyes.

But he sprang up again right away as the Wulf-farmer came a-running. Harm was on the back lawn when he heard the shouting and crying and laughing. Now he stood there, shaking throughout all his limbs, his face looking like a freshly whitewashed wall. "Wha..wha . . . what's g-going on?" he stuttered.

The preacher lifted his hand: "I'll read it out loud." Everyone held up their hands and folded them in anticipation. But not the Burvogt; he didn't have the strength for it. He stood leaning against the house, looking wretched, his mouth open and his eyes downcast, breathing heavily, as if smothering.

The preacher finished reading. Everyone laughed and cried in a mix, as if senseless. But they suddenly turned around. What was that?

The Wulf-farmer had groaned loudly and piteously, and now stood with his head against the large door, hands to his face, sobbing like a child.

He then turned and walked over to his wife as if deathly ill, took her on the arm and said weakly: "Mother, put me to bed . . . I'm so tired . . . so tired." His wife held him under the arm, wiped his tears and said: "Yes, yes . . . I'll bring you to bed, my boy. You'll get a nice good long sleep."

No one was laughing anymore. It grew very quiet, except for the children out in the meadow, who were singing a new song that they had recently learned in school:

> *"How my heart sings*
> *On a joyous summer day!*
> *Renewed, my pulse rings,*
> *The ecstasies of May!*
> *The lark is taking wing,*
> *Her bright sound o'er the dale,*
> *How lovely the little birds sing,*
> *And too, the nightingale."*

CHAPTER 13

~

The Heathland Farmers

Harm Wulf had a thorough rest indeed; he slept three and one-half weeks long, and he probably wouldn't have woken up at all, had he not had the constitution of a bear.

For he had had a nervous breakdown. It was too much for him, having to wade through blood all those years: first up to the ankles, then to the knees, then standing in it waist-deep, and rising ever higher until it was finally up past his chin. Not much more and it would have flowed into his mouth, drowning him.

For awhile now he hadn't been able to look on as a hog was being butchered, and for years he couldn't eat blood sausage. He would even feel ill whenever one of the children cut their finger.

But he had kept this all to himself and spoke about these things to no one: neither to Drewes nor Vieken, not even the preacher, let alone his wife. He had swallowed his disgust each and every day, like a dog its filth. In return for his silence, he was rewarded with hard eyes, a narrow mouth, and gray hair before his time.

And now his hair was white as snow, though he was barely fifty years old. But twenty-five years of war carried double the weight; he looked like he might already have had eighty winters behind him. He regained his health, and in many

193

ways still carried himself like a young man: he could work the
fields like a farmhand of twenty-five; he could still swing a
full scythe level with one hand; he lost not one wit of his sight
and hearing; he could still bellow and be heard on the other
side of town; he still rode like a trooper, and ate like a thresher. Nevertheless, he was an old man.

Not that his work diminished . . . quite the contrary. When
he was back on his feet, he cut building wood from the forest,
for he had promised his second son the old farm, the
Wulfstead. Not that he loved one son more than the other;
but Johanna, though she might have been his greatest love of
the three wives, was from another region - that's why she baptized her son Bartold, after her father. However, the boy who
was firstborn to him by Wieschen, he was called Harm, as the
eldest in a given generation of the Wulf clan was traditionally named. He would therefore inherit the old Wulfstead, along
with the old iron hearth kettle hook, upon which the Wolf-
rune house mark and date '1111 A.D.' was engraved. Bartold
would remain on the new farm, and eventually came to be
called Niehoff instead of Wulf; as a house brand he adopted
two Wolf-runes placed over each other, in a cross.

The old Burvogt kept his shoulder to the wheel in community affairs, too. His priority now was to provide for a church,
since the Peerhobstlers had grown accustomed to having one
of their own. It took a lot of writing and wading through official bureaucracy, but Wulf saw it through to the end.

As the preacher then asked: "But what about building
money?" the farmer replied: "I have five thousand thalers in
gold that burden me." Puttfarken understood, for he knew the
source of the wealth. Add to that the necklace of colorful
stones and pearls (which was worth nearly the same amount)
that Kasper Schewe, in his time, had found in the pocket of an
Imperial captain. Additionally, the other farmers contributed
no small sums, for their sacks of coins likewise weighed on
their hearts. Lastly, Vieken came and counted out one thousand shiny thalers in front of the preacher, saying: "This is to

make up for the scare that I gave everyone through my stu-
pidity that day against the Swedes . . . and anyhow, Trina reckoned that money such as this can't bring me luck." Thus
Ödringen got her church.

Also, the news came that the Duke had to scrape money
together for the Swedes, hence heavy taxes were to be levied.[58]
Wulf took the matter in hand and rode several times to Celle
until the issue was settled, so that the common folk wouldn't
be unfairly burdened. The Countess Meereshoffen was still
alive, though she had grown very thin and her hair totally
white, with a face as if sculpted from wax.

She enjoyed a long conversation with the Peerhobstler,
then nodded and said: "Yes, ill winds blew in those days. And
here we sit . . . not even sixty, but looking like we have eighty
years behind us! At least you have your health and wife and
children . . . I have nothing beyond a little money and all sorts
of foolish memories. But mark my word, this matter will be
settled . . . you have my hand on it!"

As he departed, she said to her niece: "Brigitta, in my entire
life I've known but two real men . . . George Iron-hand and
that fellow there!"

More than once Wulf had to prove he could still handle
things. The small work he left to Vieken and Helmke
Schierhorn; they scoured the heathlands so thoroughly that
no unwashed rabble tarried for long. Harm lived another
good stretch of years, long enough to bounce four grandchildren on his knee.

But when his wife died, he too lost his lust for life. He had
done his share, and more than his share, of work in this life;
the world could now spare him. With the passing of time, his
eyes had regained some of their lightness; but his mouth

58. One provision of the Peace of Westphalia was that the Swedish army was
to be paid 5 million thalers. Instead of leaving things solely in the hands of
the diplomats, the army sent its own representative to the congress, to insure
that Sweden's purported goal of satisfying the unpaid troops was met.

remained grim, as if worried that blood might flow into it. He died quietly, surrounded by all his children and grandchildren, along with Vieken (who still had to steal a glance at every pretty girl, though it served little purpose now) and Thedel and the preacher, who himself looked like a very old man.

It was a funeral, the likes of which had never been seen in the moorlands. All the Warwolves still living were present, as was everyone from the surrounding districts who could spare the time; the Wulfstead was black from the crowd of mourners. It was a murky day in late autumn when Harm Wulf was laid to rest, and during the ceremonial prayers the sky itself became misty.

But after the burial, as the preacher was at his pulpit delivering the eulogy (wherein he compared the man to Samson and Judas Maccabeus, who defended their people from all enemies, and although red to the neck in blood, were found worthy by God), the sun came through the clouds and shone upon all the faces. The Warwolves again grew bright of eye as they thought about those days . . . so frightening and yet still wonderful . . . when they had to ride forth with the lead billy saps hanging from their wrists. . . .

∽

To this day, there hangs a lead billy on the wall in the parlor of the Wulffstead in Ödringen, over the sofa and under a small portrait with an antique gold frame. A museum had taken great trouble to acquire the truncheon, but its owner, state representative Herman Wulff,[59] would not part with it for love or money. "If not for that, we ourselves wouldn't be here," he'd point to it and say. When strangers asked what sort of thing it was, he just shrugged his shoulders: "That's some-

59. Over the centuries, clan and family names often undergo slight changes in spelling.

thing from olden times." He told his sons, however, what he and they owed to that old truncheon with the leather strap, and why on the oldest of the family tombstones there was nothing more to see than an upright Wolf-rune.

Whenever a boy of the Wulff clan takes communion for the first time, he reads forth from the old church registry what the erstwhile Pastor Puttfarken had written about Harm Wulf on the day he died:

> "He was a hero to his folk and steadfastly defended his people from the Philistines[60] and Amalakites[61] for over twenty years during the times of the great war. May he rest in God's peace!"

The men of the Wulff clan have regained their bright eyes, but they retain their narrow lips as a legacy from Harm Wulf. All of them are not so jolly as he once was, when a young man; but he did bequeath to them his iron will. One of the ancestors became a high-ranking officer during the Wars of Liberation;[62] as reward for his service, he was to be made a titled member of the nobility, but declined: "My name suits me as is."

The main entrance of the Wulffstead still displays this proverb, carved into the crossbeam:

> "Help Yourself, Then Our Lord God Will Help You."

Those words have guided all members of the clan, past and present.

---

60. An Old Testament tribe who inhabited the maritime plain of Palestine and dominated the Israelis for forty years until their power was broken by King David.

61. The Old Testament tribe of Amalek, living on the frontiers of Egypt and Canaan, who treated the Israelites cruelly during their exodus from Egypt.

62. German spontaneous uprisings against Napoleon (1813-1814), wherein the first echoes of the quest for a unified Germany were heard, but not realized fully until 1871 under Bismarck.

Herman Wulff is a serious man who doesn't often laugh, and almost never whistles. But laugh he did, on that day when the heathland farmers elected their man to the nation's first Reichstag.[63] And on the way home that evening, he softly whistled what sounded like an old folk tune called "The Brambleberry Song."

THE END

63. Federal Parliament established upon Germany's unification as a nation in 1871.

About the Translator

ROBERT KVINNESLAND was born in New York City in 1955 to immigrant parents from Norway and Germany. He graduated summa cum laude from Trenton State College (now the College of New Jersey) in 1979 with a degree in history and German literature. He is a recipient of the German Embassy Foreign Language Poetry Award and has contributed to international historical and cultural journals.